THE BUSINESS GUIDE TO EFFECTIVE SPEAKING

THE BUSINESS GUIDE TO EFFECTIVE SPEAKING

Making presentations, using audio-viduals, and dealing with the media

Jacqueline Dunckel
Elizabeth Parnham

Self-Counsel Press
(a division of)
International Self-Counsel Press Ltd.
Vancouver
Toronto   Seattle

Printed in Canada

First edition: October, 1984
Reprinted: October, 1987; May, 1989

Cataloguing in Publication Data:

    Dunckel, Jacqueline, 1930-
    The business guide to effective speaking

    (Self-counsel series)
    ISBN 0-88908-591-9

    1. Public speaking. 2. Communication in
management. I. Parnham, Elizabeth, 1927-
II. Title. III. Series.
PN4121.D85 1984   808.5'1   C84-091161-0

Self-Counsel Press
(a division of)
International Self-Counsel Press Ltd.
1481 Charlotte Road
North Vancouver, British Columbia V7J 1H1

CONTENTS

INTRODUCTION:
LET'S TALK ABOUT SPEAKING

The theme of this book is SPEAKING IS FOR THE EAR NOT THE EYE! Whose ear? First your own. You need to hear what you're going to say. Don't wait to be surprised by the sound of your own voice expounding your ideas. Next, consider the ears of your audience. Someone who is reading and becomes confused can always go back and reread. The listener cannot do that. It's up to the speaker to guide the listener through the message.

A reader who becomes bored and disinterested can set aside the reading matter. When an audience becomes bored and disinterested, they can tune you out and think about something else. It is up to you to present your ideas in an animated, vital voice that is pleasant to the ear and demands attention. If you don't deliver your message dynamically, you might as well have it printed and mailed out. When you deliver your message with dynamic conviction, your audience will respond.

As you've been reading this, you may have noted that we've used short sentences and a number of contractions. We've been writing for the ear . . . not the eye. Too often speaking sounds like writing. You should speak to any size audience the same way you normally talk. Our experience has convinced us that too much time is spent with pencil and paper and not enough on speaking. Wonderful speeches on paper do not necessarily mean wonderful speeches when spoken.

This book is a result of our experience in the classroom, in the boardroom, and as public speakers. We have developed a unique organizational method, and it works. It is based on more speaking/less writing and allows for individuality and spontaneity while building confidence.

When we're asked, "How can you teach people to be dynamic speakers?" we're now able to say, "It's all in our book!" We've been practical and concise. We haven't used a lot of examples or illustrations. This is your "how to" book for making speeches and presentations. We have also included guidance for other speaking situations, such as dealing with the media, that require special techniques.

Make this *your* book. Follow it and become the dynamic speaker you've always wanted to be!

1

PREPARING YOUR PRESENTATION

LET'S GET ORGANIZED

Organization is the key to clarity; the key to organization is clear, logical thinking. The key to dynamic speaking is the transference of that logical thinking into a message with impact.

No matter what form of delivery you anticipate using — full outline, key word or full script — the following steps must be used as your initial plan. They are different. They require new habits. They require a flexible approach. We know they work. Remember, speaking is for the ear, not the eye. We ask you to vocalize every step — to yourself, to someone else. Hear your ideas. Get familiar with your voice and the way you express yourself. We ask you to write less, speak more, question often, and develop dynamic speaking techniques.

1. Speeches versus presentations

A general audience listening to a speaker expects to be entertained, informed or persuaded, and enjoys the unexpected. A specific audience listening to a business presentation expects explicit information, intelligent persuasion, and credible content in order to make sound decisions. Surprise and entertainment don't belong in the boardroom. That doesn't mean presentations should be dull and boring. On the contrary. They should be vital and compelling. After all, a second in the boardroom is worth as much as a second in a Las Vegas night club act.

2. Attitude

Before you start be honest with yourself about your attitude toward the

1

idea of speaking itself or toward the occasion or content of the speech or presentation. A negative attitude will permeate every aspect of organization, rehearsal, and delivery, resulting in a negative response from the audience. If you enter a presentation with the attitude that people will resist your idea, you may transmit your feelings to the audience, who will respond with the stubbornness you feared.

3. Purpose

Ask yourself, aloud, "Why am I making this speech or presentation?" If it's only because your boss told you to, that's not a good enough reason. Every speech or presentation must have a purpose. If you haven't the answer, find it. If there's no reason for making the speech or presentation, don't. You'll just be wasting your time and your audience's.

4. Audience analysis

Ask yourself, aloud, "To whom am I speaking?" You must always analyze your audience before you start any preparation. (See chapter 2.)

5. Scattergram

Write down everything you could talk about on the subject. Write randomly. Don't number your thoughts or put them in any order or form. Just empty your head and let the thoughts flow. This will start your juices flowing and release your creativity. We call this a scattergram. When you've exhausted the process, set the scattergram aside.

6. Core statement

Write out a core statement for your speech or presentation. The core statement will identify the audience, the purpose, and the expected outcome. Every speech and presentation must have a purpose. It must accomplish something. It must sell something: an idea, a concept, yourself, a product. For example: the purpose of my presentation is to convince the board that the Kauai project is both feasible and profitable.

If the operative verb in your core statement is "educate", find another one. The psychology underlying "educate" tends to make speakers talk down to their audience and lecture or speak in a paternal manner. If the verb you've chosen is "inform," be sure to include in your core statement the reason your audience needs to be informed. "Why do they need this information?" The verb inform is often a catchall allowing the speaker to go on an ego trip about what *he or she knows* rather than what *they need to know*. For best results, use dynamic verbs: persuade, convince, achieve, prove.

Say your core statement aloud to someone. Let him or her question your purpose. Be objective, not defensive. By clarifying, supporting, or changing your core statement, you will strengthen it and you'll have it clearly fixed in your mind. What you set out in your core statement you must fulfill in your speech or presentation.

7. Hidden agendas and personal interests

Having analyzed your audience and determined your purpose, now consider what questions your audience might ask — questions that could arise from hidden agendas and personal interests. Write them down. You'll want to answer as many of these questions as possible in your speech or presentation, while staying within the plan you've set for yourself. By listing the pros and cons to your core statement, you'll realize what areas need the most support. By dealing with the audience's questions within the presentation, you can eliminate being bombarded with questions from a frustrated, even angry audience at the end of your presentation.

8. Determine main points

Determine the main points of your speech or presentation by referring to your core statement and asking yourself aloud: "What does my audience need to know so I can achieve my purpose?" Refer to your scattergram. Those points are probably there. Consult your possible audience questions. You'll find points there. Imagine being able to give your audience a test after you speak. What questions would you ask to determine whether you've achieved your purpose?

Assess each point for its value in relationship to your core statement. Discard those that are not relevant. You may not use all your material because it's not needed to reach your objective and would only confuse your audience and put you overtime. Staying within your allotted time is imperative and you must be cognizant of this throughout your organization.

9. Card main points

Put your main points on 5 x 7 index cards. One point — one card. Be concise. Leave space at the top of the cards. Do not number the cards.

10. Support   Determine the support material for each main point. Your scattergram will be of assistance. You may realize you need to do research. Your support material must be accurate, honest, and factual. If you use opinion, it must be justified. Your support material should present the rationale for your point, backing it up with sound *reason*: the *evidence* for your rationale through example, illustration, comparison or analogy, statistics, testimony, and opinion.

Put your support material, concisely, under your main points on your cards.

11. Sequence main points   Under your support material restate your main point. We call this PREP — point, rationale, evidence or illustration, point (restatement). Organize your cards (main points) into a sequence based on:

(a) *Time:* suited for explaining a process, activity, historical event (1, 2, 3; past, present, future; 1910, 1930, 1950).

(b) *Space:* suited particularly to presenting geographic, physical, governmental or sectional subjects (villages, towns, cities; Canada, United States, England; kitchen, living room, bedroom).

(c) *Topical:* suited to presentation of qualities, aspects, classes, types. Suits all topics. Be careful not to make the subject too broad. Break the speech or presentation down into its component parts. (The United Nations is comprised of four parts: General Assembly, Security Council, Secretary-General, Specialized Agencies.) The topical

5

sequence is the best to use when analyzing material in relationship to people, groups or categories affected (nuclear testing, sour gas emissions, national energy policy, government cutbacks).

(d) *Problem-solution:* suited to presenting changes, getting something approved, offering a new idea or recommending a plan of action. (Problem: polluted air. Cause: combustion engine. Solution: get rid of combustion engine.) The problem-solution organization plan is very persuasive.

Do not number your cards yet. Remain flexible.

12. Transitions

Decide on the transitions you wish to use to get you from one main point to another. The form of sequence you have chosen (step #11) will determine your transitions. Use the space left at the top of your cards. Transitional words, phrases, and sentences help your audience grasp the relationship of your main points.

Examples: In the first place . . . in the second place . . . thirdly; finally; on the other hand; moreover; furthermore; as a result. Avoid overuse of next, next, next; also, also, also; now, now, now. You may use rhetorical questions to introduce new points. Questions involve the audience's mental process. In order to make a smooth transition, you may wish to provide summaries along the way to indicate that so far you have covered this point and now you are going to consider the next one. You can do this at the bottom of the cards.

Do not number your cards yet. Remain flexible.

13. Vocalize	Using your cards, vocalize your main points, support, and transitions in the order you have adopted. Get feedback from someone acting as audience-coach:

(a) Have I met the objective of my core statement through my main points?

(b) Are my main points clearly supported?

(c) Does my discussion (support) answer questions I am anticipating?

(d) Are my main points organized in a sequence that leads to a dynamic conclusion?

Add. Delete. Modify. Simplify. Rearrange. Aren't you glad you remained flexible . . . and have some blank cards left?

14. Vocalize again	Vocalize again to the same audience and consider the feedback. Refer back to your core statement. Are you achieving your purpose clearly and concisely?
15. Visual aids	Any points that need clarification, expansion or visual illustration will determine your use of visual aids. (See chapter 4.) *Visual aids should never be determined before organization.*
16. Beginning and ending	Now is the time to consider: "How do I begin and how do I end?" The beginning and ending must be related to and determined by the content and the purpose. The beginning must gain the attention of your audience and introduce them to the content. Imagine

your audience asking:

(a) Why should I listen to this?
(b) What's the subject got to do with me?
(c) What am I going to hear?

Your opening should provide all the answers. To begin a speech by saying "My business here today is to speak, yours is to listen" is not only rude, but antagonizes your audience. Your business is to speak in such a way that makes your audience *want* to listen. They are under no obligation to listen to you.

17. Beginning a speech

Speeches of a general nature may be opened with:

(a) A rhetorical question or series of rhetorical questions
(b) A story, narrative or humorous anecdote relating to or illustrating some aspect of the talk
(c) Special interest, needs or beliefs of the audience
(d) A quotation that relates to the body of the speech
(e) Startling, unusual, or curious facts related to the body of the speech
(f) A strong statement derived from the core statement and the facts within the speech

18. Beginning a presentation

The most successful method to open a business presentation is your dynamic statement of purpose and a clear plan of intent related to the sequence you chose to present your main points.

19. Concluding a speech

Conclusions must indicate to the audience: "this is the end." They must tie everything together and give a sense of finality. "Th-th-that's all folks!" is not a suitable conclusion. Neither is "I guess that's all I have to say"; "Thank you"; a shrug and a shuffle; an embarrassed smile or a duck of the head. To conclude speeches of a general nature you can:

(a) Summarize, repeat, review, or restate the theme and main points in somewhat different language than used in the body of the speech.

(b) Use methods that were used in the introduction but repeat the story, quotation, series of questions with a different twist or application.

(c) Appeal for action or belief. The appeal made to the audience's interests and needs.

20. Concluding a presentation	Closing a presentation depends on its complexity. Often a summary is needed before you can make your final conclusion which can be a recommendation, a challenge or a dynamic concluding statement. All are based on the points presented in the body of your presentation.
21. All conclusions	Never introduce new points in your conclusion.
	Be sure your conclusion relates to your beginning.
	People remember the last thing they hear the longest. Make your conclusion emphatic, forceful, and memorable. Far too many conclusions dribble off into obscurity.
	NUMBER YOUR CARDS!
22. Vocalize	Find an audience. One interested person will do. Using your cards present

everything you've done up to now, including your visual aids.

23. Checklist   Following your rehearsal use this organizational checklist:

(a) Have I examined and thought out my ideas thoroughly?

(b) Have I been objectively self-critical?

(c) Is my sequential organization logical and easy to follow?

(d) Have I attempted to cover too many points?

(e) Are my main points clearly made?

(f) Have I over-emphasized minor points?

(g) Are my supporting facts and evidence correct?

(h) Do my visual aids clarify, intensify, prolong, and deepen the audience's awareness and reinforce my main points?

(i) Have I dealt with possible audience questions and concerns?

(j) Have I fulfilled my core statement?

DELIVERY

When you have completed these steps, you are organized. You have a good solid base and should feel confident about what you have accomplished to this point. Now is the time to determine, "What method will I use to deliver my speech or presentation?"

(a) Am I confident enough to use my full content outline cards?

(b) With a few more rehearsals could I use key word cards only?

(c) Am I required to prepare and use a full text script? (Full text script is the most difficult form of delivery. See chapter

11.) You can use your cards as the outline for writing your full script. By following our method of organization you have the basis for a full text speech or presentation that you can write for the ear. If you tape your organization rehearsal (step #22), you'll find your text on the tape. You'll only have to polish.

If you must prepare a full script that will be read by board members, stockholders, fellow professionals or the media, your cards will provide the outline so you may prepare a text written for the eye. Deliver your speech or presentation from the one written for the ear.

SPEECH WRITERS

If you write speeches for others or have speeches written for you, you should go through our organizational steps with your speaker or writer. Too many speech writers have to work in limbo not knowing the purpose, the audience or the occasion. They are just told to write a speech.

Work with a tape machine and go through steps #1 to #7 together. This allows for a mutual understanding and a basis for writing the speech. It also allows the writer to hear natural phrasing, commonly used expressions, vocabulary, and rate of delivery. The writer can then capture "the flavor" of the speaker and make him or her appear natural, confident, creditable, and, most importantly, human. Too many speech writers are English majors. Too many speakers read what the English majors write . . . and read it badly. By working together — writing for the ear — you'll reap the rewards of the well-spoken word.

One final word: whether you write the speech or presentation yourself or there is a writer involved, you're communicating as a part of an organization and you must follow precedents and seek approvals, up and down. Don't surprise the very people who should be supporting you.

PRESENTATIONS TO PERSUADE

We have said that there's an element of selling in all speeches and presentations. Some presentations have a stronger need to sell, convince, win over, or change opinion. You must be prepared to use logical appeals based not only on facts but on an explanation of the facts. There are two methods of persuasion.

1. Persuasion through argument	This method requires you to be able to distinguish between fact and opinion. Facts are statements that can be measured, examined, touched, tested, and checked for reliability. Opinion is a judgment or appraisal of a situation.
2. Persuasion through motivation	This is the appeal to satisfy human needs and desires. These can be divided into self-preservation, economic security, social recognition, aesthetics, and protection of loved ones. To persuade through one of these motives you must create an awareness of a need to satisfy that motive and offer the listener a means of doing so. You can: • Present challenge. • Identify the benefits that will result from action taken. These benefits may be for the company, the department or the person taking the action. • Point out job enrichment — more responsibility, more freedom for decision, more pay.

PERSUASION PLANNING POINTS

1. Audience analysis	Analysis of your audience is most critical when you wish to persuade or change opinion.

If the majority of your audience —

- is in favor of your position,
- is subordinate to you,
- is poorly educated,
- has poor self-esteem, or
- must make a commitment publicly after you speak,

present just one side of the argument or persuade through motivation.

If the majority of your audience —

- initially disagrees with your position,
- is superior to you,
- is well-educated, or
- will be exposed later to counter-persuasion,

present both sides of the argument. Do not attempt to persuade through motivation.

Using a pro and con discussion shows the thoroughness that went into your preparation. It also takes the wind out of objections that others might raise. Be sure to include all negative arguments or you'll appear to be covering up, and you'll lose support from your audience.

When speaking to persuade, you not only tell them what you're going to tell them, tell them, and tell them what you told them, you also tell them *what to do*.

You'll be completely persuasive if the audience believes you know what you're talking about (proven facts), that you're telling the truth, and that you have the best interest of the audience (company) at heart.

Do not attempt to manipulate. Persuasion is not manipulation.

2. Competitors   Analysis of your competitors is equally important. If you can show that competitors are already doing what you're proposing, your audience may be more receptive. Most managements do not want to go with something that is absolutely new or risky. They'll accept something that's sufficiently original but not completely unfamiliar. Here are some tips for dealing with competitors.

- You'll have more success selling a new procedure that calls for only a minor change involving little cost than a radical change at a large cost.

- You can increase the value of your idea by referring to secondary, long-term, spin-off or indirect benefits or by-products. But put your main emphasis on the short-range or immediate benefits. Secondary benefits make for good support.

- Channel your idea into the direction your company is moving. Relate to problems that have high visibility. Tie it into what is currently being considered or has just been completed. Link it to management's present or past concerns.

- Sell your boss. Get your immediate superior's backing and approval. Consider his or her view when organizing your presentation. Put yourself in the boss' shoes. Imagine how you would react if the roles were reversed.

- When making a presentation to a particular group, try to convince one or two members, prior to your presentation, of the value of your idea or project. They may be able to make supporting comments or ask leading questions that will add credence to your presentation.

- Companies want to know what it will mean in dollars and cents, profit and loss. Clearly state, if possible, how your idea or project will benefit the company in dollars and cents.

- Be generous in sharing credit with others. People who have contributed to the presentation in any way may be in the audience. Their positive reaction is infectious. Using the "we" approach is the single most important ingredient in selling ideas.

- You may wish to send out an advance memo to members of the audience when speaking internally. Outline the key points of your proposed presentation and request any questions or objections. You can answer them within your presentation. Your audience is also prepared to organize their ideas before your presentation. *There is risk involved, however.* It allows the audience to be aware of your game plan in advance, and some members will hold back on questions and opinions until you make your presentation. It is imperative that your presentation receive approval and endorsement from superiors before you present it.

2
WHO'S OUT THERE?

Every book on communication will tell you there has to be a sender of the message. But if no one's listening, there's no communication happening. It's up to you, the speaker, to ensure that your audience is listening. That's why we place a great deal of importance on analyzing your audience before you start preparing your speech or presentation.

QUESTIONS TO ASK BEFORE PREPARATION

(a) Why should this audience be interested in what I have to say? What is their motivation?

(b) Are they looking forward to hearing me or is it compulsory for them to attend?

(c) What is their opinion of me? Will I have to change their opinion through my performance?

(d) What is their opinion of the subject of my speech or presentation? Do they all think alike? Will I have to win some over?

(e) What is the prevailing mood of my audience? (This question needs to be asked again on the day of your speech or presentation. Listen to the news. Keep your finger on the pulse of the people. You can't ignore disasters.)

(f) How important is my presentation to decision making?

(g) What do they expect from me?

16

(h) What do I expect from them in the way of response or action?

THE NEGATIVE AUDIENCE AND HIDDEN AGENDA

Anyone making a business presentation or political speech must recognize that members of the audience can be negative to your ideas or have a hidden agenda they want to fulfill. The larger your business organization the more likely there is to be a negative audience or hidden agenda.

1. Who could be negative to your ideas?

- People who, though not in a direct reporting relationship upward or downward from you, will be affected by whatever action you propose.
- People who see a threat to themselves or their own particular area in your proposed action.
- People who are in direct competition for dollars, space, prestige or position.

2. What do you do about a negative audience?

- As much as you can, bring out and answer the negative ideas in your presentation. That's why we ask you to consider the questions the audience might ask.
- If your speech or presentation is in opposition to their ideas, try to present both sides.
- If you can't answer all their concerns within your speech or presentation, be prepared for questions.
- Be prepared for hecklers, especially if you are a political speaker.

3. The hidden agenda

People attending small business meetings are the ones most likely to have a

17

hidden agenda. When making a presentation to a small group, or taking part in a business meeting consider:

- Who will be there?
- What particular beef, concern or axe to grind does each person have?
- What does each member of the group want to achieve personally? Recognition? Advancement? More responsibility? More of the budget?
- Have I given cause for any member of this meeting to feel threatened?

4. **What do you do about a hidden agenda?**

- As much as possible touch on a hidden agenda in your presentation, e.g., "We all realize this is a particular concern of yours, Harry." "We really appreciate the help you gave us on this project, Joe." Allay concerns, and answer ego needs as much as you can.
- Be prepared for the person who will bring out a pet peeve or concern no matter what the subject. Don't let anyone take over the discussion. Get your question period back on track.
- Be prepared for the person who will attempt to make you look bad so he or she will look good. If you can make that person look good first, he or she won't have to make you look bad. But if you can't, don't become defensive or sarcastic. Keep cool and reinforce your points.
- Be prepared to be surprised by a hidden agenda you hadn't anticipated. Remain calm. If you are making a presentation, you are responsible for the course of the meeting.

5. Final word on hidden agendas

Whenever you attend a meeting, consider who will be there. What could be their hidden agendas? What could you be asked about that doesn't appear on the agenda? Be prepared to present your own "hidden" agenda.

AUDIENCE ANALYSIS FOR PUBLIC SPEAKING SITUATIONS

Answer these questions to analyze your audience

(a) How large is the group?
(b) What is the age range of the audience?
(c) Do they have a common interest?
(d) What is the educational range of the audience?
(e) What is their economic background?
(f) Is it a racially mixed audience?
(g) Is there a political factor involved?
(h) What is the male/female ratio?
(i) What benefit can they gain from me?
(j) Does the occasion of my speech have some special significance to this audience?

WILL YOUR AUDIENCE GET YOUR MESSAGE?

After analyzing your audience, you must consider the "language" of your speech or presentation.

(a) Will everyone understand highly technical terms?
(b) Do I need to paraphrase or give an explanation? Never talk down to an audience or tell them, "You won't know what this means so I'll explain it for you." Instead use terms like "as we all know that is . . . ."
(c) Don't try to impress your superiors by flaunting your knowledge. They

want straightforward information in order to reach decisions. They hired you for your expertise. You don't have to redo your Ph.D. every time you make a presentation.

(d) Do not use terms, illustrations, or examples that will offend any member of your audience because of race, sex, religion or nationality.

JOKES, STORIES, ANECDOTES, AND ILLU-STRATIONS

- Don't tell a joke to warm up the audience. A joke must be directly related to your subject matter.

- Don't tell jokes in a business presentation. Your audience is looking for information not entertainment. This doesn't mean that presentations shouldn't be palatable and made with a sense of showmanship. They should be.

- Don't ever tell jokes, if you can't. Very few people tell jokes well.

- Don't tell a joke, story, anecdote or use an illustration if it will offend anyone in your audience because of its language or subject matter.

  Only Polish people should tell jokes or stories about Polish people. Only women etc.

  I'm sure you get our point. You can antagonize and lose an audience if you don't follow this advice.

3

WHEN AND WHERE WILL YOU SPEAK?

Whenever you make a speech or presentation, you should know exactly when and where you will be speaking whether it is in-house or miles away.

QUESTIONS TO ASK

(a) How large is the space?

(b) What is the set up of the room?

(c) Can it be changed to accommodate me?

(d) What audio-visual equipment is available?

(e) Is there power if I want to use other or additional audio-visual equipment?

(f) Can the room be darkened if necessary?

(g) If I need to use a microphone, what is available? (See section on microphones.)

(h) What time do I speak?

(i) How long am I expected to speak?

(j) What is the format, agenda or order?

(k) Do I follow or precede other speakers? If so, are they speaking on the same subject or making a presentation on a complementary or opposing aspect?

(l) Who is my contact person? Is this person responsible for equipment, seating arrangements, having the room open on time?

(m) Will people be drifting in and out while I talk?

BEST TIMES TO SPEAK

Here are some tips on the best time to speak. You won't always have a choice, but if you do you can use these ideas.

- The best time to speak is first thing in the morning.
- As you approach coffee break interest wanes.
- As you approach lunch, audience attention is focused on the prospects of food. After lunch, audience attention is focused on digesting same. Showing slides and films in a darkened room after lunch invites people to sleep. If your audience has been drinking, they can be inattentive, argumentative or sleepy.
- Speaking after dinner gives you the problems of subdued lighting, full stomachs, predinner cocktails, and dinner wine. Speaking at lunch gives you the additional problem of people concerned with getting back to work. Dinner and luncheon speakers should keep it short, keep it moving, and keep it interesting.

HOW LONG TO SPEAK

- Don't feel because you have been given 45 minutes to speak that you must speak for 45 minutes. If you can put across what you have to present in 20 minutes, do so.
- Audiences today have been raised on television. Segments of 10, 20, or 30 minutes are acceptable. Executives hearing one presentation after another welcome the short, succinct presentation.

CHECK THE LOCATION WHERE YOU'LL SPEAK

- Check sight lines. Will your visual aids be seen by the audience?
- Check windows. Can the drapes be pulled to keep out light and distracting movement?

- Is the room unusually hot or cold? Can a problem be rectified?
- If there's a podium or lectern and you plan to use it, try it out. If it is too low, find a way to build it up so your head isn't dropping down. If it blocks out most of your body, bring your own soap box to stand on.
- Check for other distractions: noisy air conditioners, fans, people in the hall outside.
- Be sure the room is set up so that people entering the room late can come in at the back.
- Be sure no door opens onto the area where you are making your speech or presentation.
- Find out where the nearest bathroom is.
- If you need to have a glass of water near at hand, make sure it's available.

ADDITIONAL CONSIDERA- TIONS — SPEECHES, PRESENTING PAPERS

- Will the press be there? If so, you must consider what they might perceive to be controversial. Be sure you have included some good 15 or 20 second quotes in your speech or presentation. (See chapter 13.)
- Will you be taped? Will the tapes be distributed? You must give written permission. Decline if you wish.

4

LET'S LOOK AT VISUAL AIDS

A visual aid is anything the audience sees that aids them in understanding or believing points you want to make.

Most business presentations incorporate the use of visual aids because of the combined impact of the vocal and the visual. The great danger is that presenters place the major emphasis on visual aids and relegate themselves to the minor role of narrator or technician.

You are central to the presentation. It needs you, your interpretation, your explanation, your conviction, and your justification. Otherwise, why are you there? Don't prove to the company that it can get along without you.

Because visuals are so central to presentations they are often in the hands of the inexperienced. When you do use visual aids, know how to use them with confidence and ease. Don't lose credibility by being under-rehearsed.

VALUE OF VISUAL AIDS TO THE PRESENTER

- Visual aids increase your motivation and enthusiasm.
- They increase your confidence — when you are well-rehearsed.
- Their choice and preparation makes you think clearly and carefully.
- When chosen properly they strengthen the organization of your preparation and support your purpose.
- They help you to increase the audience's enthusiasm for your project.
- They allow you to move and act more spontaneously.

24

VALUE OF VISUAL AIDS TO THE AUDIENCE

- They reduce confusion, misunderstandings, and inaccuracies.
- They provide clarity to abstract concepts.
- They emphasize and reinforce key concepts of an idea.
- They deepen and vitalize audience involvement.
- They stimulate imagination and empathetic listening.
- They provide clarity to technical procedures.
- They generate and hold attention.
- They create a more lasting impression.

WHEN TO USE VISUAL AIDS

Use visual aids when:

- It is difficult to visualize the idea, concept or procedure.
- There are divergent opinions and viewpoints.
- Statistical or numerical data is involved.
- Engineering or production details are used.
- Geophysical, medical or other scientific data or procedures are being presented.
- A radical new product, service or procedure is proposed.
- Structural details and relationships have to be shown.
- You want your audience to retain material for a length of time. Visuals increase retention up to 95%.
- You are explaining operations, machines, physical or natural events.
- A working model cannot be brought to a meeting.

- You want to show organizational relationships.
- You want to summarize factual material.

WHAT VISUAL AID SHOULD YOU USE?

1. Slides
- Less text is needed if slides are well chosen.
- Disadvantages: dark room means loss of audience contact; some loss of flexibility.

2. Overhead or viewgraph
- Most effective visual aid for small audiences. Room doesn't have to be darkened. You can maintain eye contact, draw on or overlay transparencies.
- They are economical. It takes one hour to do a visual that would take four hours to produce as a slide. No waiting for photo lab processing.
- Disadvantages: audience blocking of image, image dancing on the screen, keystoning of image.

3. Opaque
- You can show pictures in books and flat objects.
- Disadvantages: dark room, noisy machine.

4. Tape
- For music, actual quotes, sound effects. Can be stopped and started smoothly if tape is marked and volume preset.

5. Chalkboard and whiteboard
- Most effective when you want to build step by step with explanation. Your audience can see only what

26

you present and not "explore" the whole diagram.

- Disadvantages: takes time. You must be able to speak and write at the same time. Your writing must be legible and your drawings clear.

6. Film and video

- Can be used as part of a speech or presentation.
- Disadvantages: dark room. Loss of audience contact which has to be regained.

7. Charts

- More effective than chalkboards. You can keep your eyes on the audience. You can use color and drawings.
- Disadvantages: time needed to prepare clear, neat charts. Keeping them in order.

8. Flip charts

- All in one. You can use them to build an idea.
- Disadvantages: flipping can cause problems. Suggest you work backwards and flip pages down.

9. Maps

- Put an area into immediate orientation. Show only what serves your purpose. Leave out details that confuse.

10. Graphs

- Use when presenting numbers and quantity in relationship to time. The graph is the eye of statistics and allows for quick comprehension.

11. Handouts

- Don't — until the end of your speech or presentation. If you have material you wish to refer to put it on a viewgraph, slide, chalkboard or chart. If this is not possible, hand out only the material you are discussing and hand it out at that point in your presentation, not before. Otherwise, you provide a distraction from your speech or presentation.

WHAT IS A GOOD VISUAL AID?

- *Visible:* The audience must be able to see it. The operative word is visual.
- *Audible:* Audio aids must be heard and understood by the audience.
- *Accurate:* Make diagrams to scale; don't exaggerate.
- *Appropriate:* The aid should aid not confuse or detract.
- *Clear:* Keep them simple with clean, clear lines and bright, unmuddied color.
- *Neat:* All visuals should be neat. Wash chalkboards. Clean type. Use presentable equipment.
- *Efficient:* Prepare exhibits in advance. Keep visual aids hidden until ready for use. Have projector focused. Test equipment in advance.

Good visual aids amplify and clarify meaning. If they attract attention to themselves, they detract from the presentation.

Do not put your notes onto flip charts, transparencies, or slides. They may be a crutch for you but do not aid your audience.

USING AIDS

Any *visual* device needs a *verbal* setting if its point is to be understood. Tell audiences what it is they are looking at. State first what the visual aid is intended to show. Point out its main features so the audience may grasp the whole of the slide. Use these techniques for effective use of visual aids.

- Pointing is necessary to direct the focus of the audience. With slides and viewgraphs you can give an overall view with one and then use subsequent slides or transparencies to zero in on a particular aspect. Split slides may also be used. (These will be discussed later.)

- Always stand to the side of the aid.

- When demonstrating, hold the aid up and out.

- Don't let your head drop down or turn too far to the side or audibility is lost.

- Don't turn your back to the audience.

- Don't stand in front of the aid.

- Don't play with the aid, pointer or chalk.

- Don't talk to your visual aid. Look no more than one-fourth of your time at your visual aid — to focus audience attention on it. The rest of the time you should be looking at your audience. The audience's eyes, not yours, are kept on visual materials. You must be constantly reading your audience.

- Use the hand nearest the visual aid for pointing, and keep the foot nearest to the aid ahead of the other foot. This keeps the body from turning into the aid and away from the audience.

- Keep visual aids out of the hands of the audience. Passing aids creates a distracting ripple through the audience and a loss of attention to the speaker.
- Don't pass out handouts unless you're going to have the audience use them with you.
- Use aids in a lively, dynamic fashion.
- Don't let the aid be a signal before using it or after you are through with it. Keep the cover on; put it back on after (black slides, covered charts, etc.).
- Arrange for someone to turn lights on and off.
- Rehearse realistically with your visual aids. You will bore, exasperate, and anger your audience if you handle visual materials ineptly. Misused audio-visuals can destroy a presentation.
- Plan how you're going to set up and take down visual aids.
- If running the equipment becomes a hassle, get someone else to assist you. Rehearse with your assistant. Work out script signals. You don't want to be saying "next slide please" throughout.
- Don't count on anyone else; check everything beforehand. The more audio-visuals you use the more risk you take of something going wrong. Murphy's Law constantly proves itself when using visual aids.
- Don't get enchanted with gimmicks. Lighted pointers and multi-

media extravaganzas very often call attention to themselves and do not help your audience understand what you are trying to put across. They detract rather than support.

- Be prepared to make a presentation if the visual aids fail.

1. Using the chalkboard and whiteboard

- Keep the board clean.
- Erase all unrelated material.
- Have erasers and extra chalk or markers available. (Be sure your markers are those specifically for whiteboard use.)
- Break chalk in half if it squeaks.
- Check lighting; avoid glare.
- Present material simply, briefly, and concisely. Limit writing to key phrases. Think in terms of restraint.
- Write legibly and neatly. Letters should be about three inches high.
- Leave space between lines.
- Use colored chalk or markers for emphasis.
- Underline for emphasis.
- Combine printing and longhand for emphasis.
- Predraw difficult diagrams lightly and trace during presentation.
- Use a pointer to direct audience attention to major points.
- Do not play with chalk or marker between writing. Put it down.
- Allow time for the audience to read, study, and copy developed material.
- Stand to the side of material being presented. Remove all obstructions.

2. Using a prepared flip chart

- Have a rough draft to ensure all points are covered. (Each page should be carefully made, not thrown together.)
- Keep it simple. Limit to one idea per chart.
- Use key words or phrases. No more than nine lines per chart, seven words per line.
- Charts should follow rules of all visual aids to clarify.
- Use no more than 32 charts per hour.
- Write or print legibly in large, clear, uncrowded letters.
- Leave space between lines.
- Use color for emphasis, not decoration.
- Underline words for emphasis.
- Avoid use of legends, abbreviations, and acronyms.
- Make facts and figures stimulating to your audience.
- Follow the rules of slide making for making graphs, maps, etc.
- Use charts to reinforce main points and summarize.

3. Making foils and viewgraphs

- If you make your viewgraph masters on 8½ x 11 sheets they should be readable from 10 feet away.
- If you make last minute viewgraphs, do not produce them in standard type on an 8½ x 11 sheet. Prepare them by printing on the celluloids using a felt pen. The felt tip will keep you from printing too small. Use the 10-foot test to make sure they can be read.
- You should not put any more on a viewgraph than you would on a

slide. They are both projected onto a six-foot surface.

- If you need to show a viewgraph more than once, make two copies so you don't have to go back and forth.
- Refer to the section on making slides; the same rules apply to making viewgraphs.

4. Using the overhead

- Check working condition of the projector.
- Rehearse with the same projector you will be using.
- Always have an extra bulb available.
- Focus the projector before presentation.
- Lower some room lights if needed.
- Arrange the seating so that no one's view is obstructed by the arm of the overhead.
- Avoid keystoning by tilting the screen forward to accommodate the low position of the projector. If possible, use a rear screen projection or a long-throw projector.
- Stand or sit to the side of the projector. Maintain eye contact with the audience.
- Use a pointer (on screen) but don't become a part of the picture. Use a pencil or pointed swizzle stick on the foil to direct audience attention.
- Use a sheet of paper to cover undeveloped material on the foil. This prevents the audience from getting ahead of you.
- Use overlays to build complicated material.

- Continue to talk as you change foils. You can summarize what you've just shown and make the transition to the next foil.

- When you change foils or transparencies, hold the next one in one hand while quickly pulling the used one away with the other. Some projectors have a device that turns the light off automatically during changes.

  If you don't want to turn the projector off between transparencies, cover the transparency table of the projector with black paper when you are not using it.

- For very polished performances you can use two projectors simultaneously. Put them close together and train their projection onto the same image area. In use, one projector is off and loaded with the next foil. When you want that foil, the projector is turned off and the other turned on quickly so there is an image on the screen at all times. (This requires team work and much rehearsal. We recommend you use slides instead.)

- Remove foil immediately after discussion to prevent distraction. As you remove foils, turn them over and lay them one on top of the other in order, keeping them well segregated from those you will be using.

- Watch for curling or browning foils caused by a very hot projector or a foil left on the projector too long. This does not occur as much as it did in the past, but can still happen.

- Be sure your foils or transparencies are marked or numbered so that you can tell immediately (without holding them up to the light or putting them on the projector) what they are and if they are in order.
- Turn off the projector when you are finished.

5. Using slides

- Slides allow you to extend the descriptive power of your words by giving visual examples of exactly what the words mean.
- Slides should not take the place of careful preparation and good delivery. They are an extension of your meaning, not a substitute for you as a speaker.
- If the slides have more importance than your presence, personal experience, and knowledge, make a slide tape presentation that can be presented by a technician.
- Do not put the words of your presentation on slides. It may assist you, but no audience wants to read along with the bouncing ball. You are insulting their intelligence.

MAKING SLIDES

- Confine the slide to material that can be seen from every seat in the house. When sketching your ideas on 8½ x 11 sheets be sure they are readable from 10 feet away. A 35mm slide should be readable from two feet (arm's length).
- Use only those features and details essential for clarity. Avoid all useless labels and names on charts, graphs or maps. Labels must be

large so they can be read. Horizontal labeling is more readable than vertical labeling.

- Slides should not have elaborate or decorative use of line and color. They should communicate information, not show you have an artist in your graphics department.

1. Designing slides working with the graphics department

Speak with the designer only after you have organized your presentation and know where you want to use a slide for clarification. *Know what is to be depicted on each slide and why.*

- Evaluate each proposed slide with the designer.
- Determine, once again, if there is need for a slide at all. Each slide should have a significant reason for use. Do not use slides prepared for another presentation just because you have them.
- Determine if the audience can understand and absorb the information from the slide in the time they have to see it. One slide, one idea, one minute. Use more than one slide per minute if you're taking a visual sight-seeing trip through a process or facility.
- Do you have too many slides saying too little or too few saying too much?
- Are your suggested ideas for the designer just that — suggestions? The designer should be free to develop fresh and imaginative solutions, but you must be free to veto slides that are works of art but do

not accomplish their task. Have a mutual base of understanding concerning lettering, color, and design.

- Are there copyright problems? Don't ask a designer or graphic department to use copyright material — photographs, diagrams or text from magazines or books. Let them develop material for you if there is a problem.

- Can your writing and diagrams be easily read and understood? The designer shouldn't be expected to be a magician. Be sure the material you give them to work with is clear.

- Use fewer numbers along coordinate axes than you would for a report. Your audience can't turn the screen to read as they can a report.

- Check all spelling, grammar, and terminology before you give it to the designer or graphics department.

- Check your script and slides with the designer. Don't try to give two messages at once. The designer may find that you're putting complex material in the script that needs clarification through the eye (slide).

2. **Selecting typeface**

- Choose typeface with the designer. Be consistent.

- Use sans serif type. Serif type lacks clarity when projected through small, narrow openings. Helvetica, Helvetica Medium, Univers 55, and Univers 65 are excellent type styles.

- Once you select your typeface, use it exclusively for that particular presentation. Within the typeface are a range of weights and itali that will fulfill all your typographi needs.

- Fancy typefaces and script shoul be avoided. Their over-designe character is inappropriate for th informational purpose of you slides.

- Normal letter spacing should b used. Tight spacing can be very dif ficult to read, particularly on rev ersed slides where they tend t fuzz.

- Flush-left type is simpler and easie to read. Use it consistently instea of centered lines of type. Usin one-line spacing and a differen weight of type is better tha indenting material.

- Type set entirely in capital letters i harder to read than type set i upper and lower case letters.

- Color, rather than capitals or italics can be used for emphasis.

- Two sizes of type are usually al that's necessary for most presenta- tions.

- Type that's readable at 7 yards may be difficult to read at 15 yards and impossible at 30.

- Red type is completely legible in a completely dark room, but may be impossible to read at half the dis- tance in a room with some ambient light.

- Red, blue, magenta, and green type can be very difficult to read under certain light conditions. ("Surprise Blue" sometimes projects as pink.)

- White backgrounds produce a glare.
  White type on black can also glare.

3. Use of weight

Before talking with your designer, you should have an understanding of what line and weight can do for your slides.

- The width of lines can make for distinctiveness and emphasis.
- A wide or heavy line should be used for the chief feature, for example, the curve of a graph.
- A medium weight line should be used for a less significant feature, for example, the boundaries or ordinate and abscissa of a graph.
- A light weight or narrow line should be used for a background feature, for example, the squares of a graph if the graph needs squares.
- When there are two features of the same importance, a solid line is used for one, a broken line for the other.
- Similar considerations should govern the size and weight of labels and lettering.

4. Use of color

Before working with your designer you should have an understanding of the psychology of color and how to use it in preparing slides.

- You can do a thorough audience analysis and find out which color is preferred by the people you want to influence most.
- We are *preconditioned* to red — stop; green — go; amber — yield. You may use these colors as signals and

take advantage of this preconditioning.

- *Warm colors:* red, yellow, gold, brown, bright green, orange.
- *Cool colors:* blue, grey, light green, pastels.

  You may use colors to get an audience to react warmly or coolly to an idea or project.

- *Fire-engine yellow* is the color the eye will go to first, followed by white and clear red.

- *Pastels:* a general reaction is that they are feminine or wishy-washy. Do not choose them for a strong idea.

- *Shades or hues:* you are best to use primary colors and strengths within them. Muddy hues impress as muddy, unclear ideas and concepts.

- Use no more than three colors unless your graph, chart, figure or table has more than three features.

- Use contrasting colors. (These are in the regions of the primary hues: red or red-orange, bright blue, bright green, and yellow-green.

- Use the same color for the same feature whether the feature is repeated in the same diagram or chart or appears on successive slides.

- Use white, light green, light yellow or light blue against a dark background.

- Use black, red, dark blue, or dark green against a white or grey background.

5. Using split slides

Split slides can be used to present two, three, or four images at once. They allow you to show relationships, direct focus, and put things into perspective for an audience. We caution you not to overuse as it can split the audience's focus and can also become gimmicky. Discuss with the designer. Don't use just because it is something new.

- Discuss with the designer if you want to use more than one projector . . . and why. If it's so an image can remain on and be referred to (a map for example) while you are discussing other relationships, it might be advantageous. Don't use just because everyone else does.

- Be sure to proofread and check all information after the designer has completed the art work. It takes two to proofread with accuracy: one reading aloud from the original while another checks the art work.

- Be sure to use the original slides rather than duplicates. Each successive copy becomes darker and muddier.

- Computer graphic equipment is being used by more and more graphic departments. It allows you to make changes on the spot; it updates old presentations and produces slides more quickly. But the computer can't do everything. It is used mainly for charts, graphs, maps or type slides. It cannot make cartoons or other illustrations. If your graphics department is using computer graphic equipment, discuss its possibilities before you plan your graphics.

41

SPECIAL CONSIDERATIONS FOR SLIDES

- When making presentations or presenting papers, make your first slide a title slide. It should include the names of all the contributors. Giving credit is very important.

- You can make your second slide a brief outline of your presentation or the purpose of your presentation or paper. This helps the audience recognize immediately where you are taking them.

- Have a succinct concluding slide (tell them what you told them). The last thing your audience hears they will remember the longest. If you reinforce it with the visual it will be remembered even longer.

- If you need to show a slide more than once, put in a second copy.

- Never include a slide just to add a little humor. It can be so distracting that you will lose your audience for the rest of your presentation.

Slide check list

(a) If more than one slide is used, does the figure/table/graph have an identification number?

(b) If the answer is "yes" to (a), does the word figure, table or graph precede the identification number?

(c) If the answer is "yes" to (a), are Arabic or Roman numerals used consistently?

(d) Is the figure/table/graph given a title?

(e) If the answer is "yes" to (d), is the title complete? Does it tell the viewer what information will be provided?

(f) Is a source line used (either at top or bottom)?

(g) Is a date of source used?

(h) If color is not used, would color help emphasize points?

(i) If color is used, are the colors easily distinguishable from one another?

(j) If color is used, are the right colors used to give emphasis to that material to be emphasized?

(k) Is lettering (words, letters, numbers) large enough for the audience in the last row to read easily?

(l) Are words, letters, numbers, rows, and columns separated by lines or by enough space to be read easily?

(m) Does lettering have professional appearance?

(n) Are all words correctly spelled?

(o) If the significance of colors or symbols has to be understood, is a key provided?

(p) If "yes" to (o), does the key provide adequate information for the understanding of the slide?

(q) Does the design promote understanding of the data?

(r) Does the slide contain any information not necessary for the understanding of the data?

(s) Are pictures, charts, and bar graphs used for greater clarity? (Line graphs are more difficult to understand.)

CHECKLIST FOR USING VISUAL AIDS

(a) Have I chosen the right visual for the subject, the audience, and the room, or have I decided to use all slides just because it's expected or everyone else does?

(b) Have I underestimated the intelligence of my audience by using tiny

43

tot or read-along-with-Dick-and-Jane visuals? Am I using my visuals merely as a cue card for myself? (If so, get rid of them. Use key word notes for yourself.)

(c) Have I considered the cost and time my visuals will take to make? Do I have the funds and the time needed to allow for preparation and rehearsal?

(d) Have I simplified my ideas so they can be demonstrated clearly?

(e) Do my visuals clarify or merely support? (If they merely support, don't use.)

(f) Do my visuals have a consistent basic structure and unity?

(g) Have I put too much material on one visual? One idea per visual is the rule.

(h) Is there anything on the visual that is not pertinent to the point being presented?

(i) Does the eye go to the most important concept on the visual through choice of color, typeface, and line or does the eye jump around because of false signals?

(j) Are my visuals free from complicating typefaces, art techniques, and symbols?

(k) Can my audience easily grasp what they see? Are my visuals direct and to the point?

(l) Do my visuals give pertinent information without distortion?

(m) Can my visuals be seen from any point in the audience?

(n) Have I presented my visuals on an audience?

(o) Have I planned two to four rehear-sals with my visuals before I make my presentation?

(p) Is the equipment available for the day of my presentation?

(q) Have I made a solid booking for the equipment I'll need?

5

LET'S HEAR WHAT YOU HAVE TO SAY: REHEARSING

Too many speeches and presentations remain on the paper or in the heads of the speakers or presenters until the day they are to be given. Rehearsal is vitally important whether you are using a full content outline, key notes or full text.

HOW TO REHEARSE

- Rehearse to remember ideas, not words.
- Do not memorize! By rehearsing you will become familiar with the material.
- Rehearse aloud.
- Push yourself through the entire speech or presentation during each rehearsal.
- If you are using visual aids, always rehearse with them.
- Rehearse with an audience whenever possible.
- Rehearse with someone who can be an audio editor and give you an honest critique of your performance.

1. Eye contact

Make eye contact with your audience. Knowing the size of the audience you'll be addressing, rehearse making contact with every segment. If the audience is large, mentally divide the room into four and let your eyes move from the middle of one quarter to the middle of another. It will appear that you are looking at everyone within the quarter.

With small groups, try to include all individuals in your gaze at some time during your speech or presentation.

2. Gestures

Let gestures happen naturally. If they are motivated by what you are saying, they will be right. Never practice gestures. They'll be contrived and phony. Large, strong, positive gestures reinforce your points. Remember, you are the best visual aid there is.

Don't be afraid of motivated movement. You don't have to stand static in one spot. Nor do you want to pace randomly. Changing your stance, moving in on a strong idea, taking a couple of steps while pausing can add drama and release tension.

3. Pauses

Use pauses. Pauses are powerful and should be plentiful. You need a pause to gather your thoughts. Your audience needs a pause to think about what you've said and to get ready for what you'll say next. Your audience is dealing with a vocal message. You have to provide thought time. This is especially true when delivering a speech or presentation from a full text.

4. Timing

Time your rehearsals. Stay within your allotted time. Don't speed up your delivery. Take out extraneous material. Tighten your content. Speakers and presenters should use a slower rate of delivery than in ordinary speech.

5. Taping

Tape-record one or two rehearsals. Place the microphone about three feet away so you're able to get a taping of a natural delivery. Listen for vocal vitality, identification of main points, and clarity of voice and purpose.

Videotape one or two rehearsals. View yourself objectively. (See video checklist.)

6. Image

Do not use a mirror in rehearsal. We've found that people tend to look into their own eyes. Because you are seeing it as you are doing it, it is difficult to separate one from the other. It is hard to be objective when looking into a mirror. We tend to see what we want to see.

Rehearse in your speech clothes so you feel comfortable and confident in them.

CHECKLIST FOR VIEWING YOURSELF ON VIDEOTAPE

(a) Did I have good eye contact? Did I include all members of my audience?

(b) Did I sound alive, interested, concerned?

(c) Did I appear relaxed, yet vital?

(d) Did my ideas progress smoothly, logically?

(e) Were my main points identifiable?

(f) Was the purpose of my presentation or speech achieved?

(g) Were my gestures free and meaningful?

(h) Did I telegraph any nervousness to the audience through mannerisms, movement or voice?

(i) Did I use any qualifying words that weakened my points (perhaps, possibly, maybe)?

(j) Did I speak at an overall rate that was fast enough so that it was not boring, but not so fast that my

48

audience had to work to keep up to me?

(k) Did I vary my rate using a slower pace for more important ideas or reinforcement of ideas?

(l) Did I speak clearly? My audience must not only hear me, they must understand what I'm saying.

(m) Did I use my visual aids easily and confidently?

(n) Did my clothes project the proper image?

(o) Did my grooming project the proper image?

6

HOW DO YOU SOUND?

English speaking audiences respond positively to rich, deep, well-modulated, dynamic voices that carry conviction and credibility. Very few people recognize their own voices, for the voice you hear from inside is not the voice the audience hears. When you hear your voice on tape, you're apt to say, "That doesn't sound like me!" You dismiss the sound of your voice and don't give it the attention it deserves. You must realize that your voice is the instrument that carries your spoken message. As important as your message may be, it can be marred if your voice is unpleasant to the listeners' ears. Voice blemishes can destroy or shatter an otherwise appealing image. They can rob you of power, authority, and persuasion.

HOW TO EVALUATE YOUR VOICE

- Recognize that the voice you hear on a good tape or video recorder is the voice that people hear.
- Be objective and recognize the fact that voices cannot be changed, but they can be improved.
- Realize that your voice is distinctive to you — as distinctive as your fingerprints.
- Isolate and become aware of the blemishes that may keep your voice from being as pleasant and powerful as it might be.

1. Are you a nose talker, a honker (nasal)?

When you talk through your nose, you twang. Test yourself by clasping your nose between your thumb and forefinger. Say: "She sang seventeen songs and swooned." Your fingers will pick up the vibration caused in your nose by "m," "n," and "ng," the only

50

nasal sounds in the English language. Hold your nostrils and say, "woe, oh woe, oh woe." The sound should come entirely from your mouth. Try "sow, sow," and "low, low". Again the sound comes from the mouth. If you buzz or feel the sound trying to come through the nose, even on "o" or the "1," you are a nose talker.

2. Are you a shrieker (strident, shrill)?

Look at yourself in the mirror as you speak. Does your neck look taut? Do the veins and cords stand out like ropes? Are the muscles around your chin tight to the eye and the touch? If they are, you probably sound like a seagull. Try tying a ribbon around your neck, at the level of your Adam's apple. If you feel the ribbon choking you as you approach the end of each sentence, your voice is strident and forced. Many female newscasters have nasal, strident, unpleasant voices. They're mistaking a forced sound for an authoritative sound.

3. Are you there (lack of projection)?

Do you sound weary and depressed? Do you constantly have to repeat because people do not hear you? Do people take what you have to say seriously or do they think you are cute (an adjective usually applied to women)? Place a finger on your Adam's apple and say "Zzzzzz." You'll feel a buzz. It is a voiced sound which means the vocal cords are in vibration. Place your finger on your Adam's apple and say, "Sssss." Your larynx doesn't vibrate. It is the unvoiced whispered counterpart of "zzzz." With your finger still on your larynx, make a remark in your normal voice. If the telltale buzz is missing, you're probably a whisperer. Many sex symbol starlets affect a breathy voice which they feel enhances the symbol. But that's not the image you want.

4. Are you a fader (unsupported breath)?

A close relative to the whisperer is the fader. If you start sentences with enough volume and vitality but fade off at the ends of sentences, your voice is not well supported and your breathing is probably high in the chest when it should be in the middle of the body.

5. Do you mumble?

A mumbler, like a whisperer, manages to keep secrets even when trying to reveal them. If you run words together, omitting whole syllables, you're a mumbler. Your lips and tongue are lazy. Speak into a mirror. If your lips barely move, you're mumbling. You know for certain that you mumble when people mistake what you said for something else.

6. Do you have lockjaw (tension in the jaw)?

If your jaw is tense, your mouth can't open to let the sound out. Your tongue can't move freely to make crisp, clear consonants. A tight jaw contributes to a mumbled sound. Check your mirror once again. Does your mouth open when you speak or do the words have to make their way past clenched teeth.

7. Are you a foghorn (hoarse and raspy)?

If your throat tires quickly when you talk; if you're constantly trying to clear it; if you're constantly hoarse even though you don't have a cold, don't smoke, and are told by a doctor that there is nothing organically wrong with your throat, you're not using your breath properly to support your voice.

The result is a fuzzy, foggy, or grating sound that irritates the listener's ears as well as your throat. Excessive shouting (as opposed to projecting) can produce a hoarse, raspy voice. Cheerleaders, drill sergeants, coaches, and campaigning politicians often have the foghorn problem.

8. Monotonous?   There is no such thing as a monotone voice — speaking on one note. But there are certainly boring voices. The average speaking voice runs a scale of 12 to 20 notes. Unfortunately, some people use only about five of them. If you are one of those, your voice has all the fascination of a worn-out faucet — you drip, drip, drone; others doze. Record yourself in conversation. Record yourself speaking formally and reading aloud. Do you vary the pitch, the pacing, the emphasis according to the sense? Or does every sentence sound like the one before? Does every word sound like another? Does each sentence end on the same note?

9. Do you speak too fast — too slow (rate)?   Do you speak so quickly that people give up trying to keep up? Or do you find that others often complete sentences for you rather than wait until you finish? People speak an average of 150 words per minute. You must take the comments of your listeners seriously. What may seem right to you may be far too fast or too slow for the listener, who must receive the message. Rapid rate coupled with poor articulation and accent or dialect can make understanding impossible. A slow rate of speech in a hot climate seems natural, but listeners in a cold climate will become impatient.

10. Do you have a speech mustache?

Speech mustaches are untidy additions you don't need. They're the mispronunciations, verbalized pauses, non-phrases, incorrect sounds, and tag ends. Speech should be clean-shaven. Saying gonna for going to, gist for just; fillum for film and idear for idea are speech mustaches. "Um" and "ah" may fill a pause but they don't mean anything except that you left your motor running. You know, like, okay, right and eh give away the fact that you're unsure of yourself and your speech mustache is badly overgrown.

11. Do you speak with a dialect or have an accent?

Every country has regional dialects. England abounds in them. Americans can quickly identify Texans, New Englanders, and New Yorkers. Newfoundlanders, Quebeckers and southern Albertans have distinctive Canadian dialects. They all speak English but the region has a particular identifying sound. The influx of immigrants to English speaking countries has produced accented speech. The "th" sound is substituted with "t," "d," "s," "z" or "f." The "l" and "r" sounds may be reversed or replaced with "o." "V" and "w" may be reversed and final "ed's" missing. Dialects and accents can be charming and distinctive. However, if they interfere with the communication process, you should consider working to clarify sounds.

HOW TO IMPROVE YOUR VOICE

The act of speaking is an "overlaid" process. You're using many groups of muscles to produce sound. Improvement can be made through a regular corrective program, as the problems we've just outlined are due mostly to bad habits.

However, before you start a voice improvement program, you should check with your doctor to ensure that you do not have any physical problems such as diseased adenoids, polyps or throat infections. (Never let a sore throat go beyond two weeks without seeking medical advice.)

If you have to constantly clear your throat or you find it difficult to swallow, see your physician. Only a registered speech therapist should advise concerning problems such as stuttering or other vocal problems caused by injury or trauma.

1. Nasality

You must learn to relax your jaw and tongue so you can open your throat and mouth letting the sound out through the mouth instead of shunting it out through the nose.

Do the following exercises:

(a) Yawning is the absolute exercise for this problem. Learn to yawn at will, under any circumstances. With eyes gently closed, bring your lips together lightly. Drop your jaw loosely, lips still closed. Let a big, lazy yawn take over, opening your mouth and the back of the throat w-i-d-e; feel the stretch, up and sideways, of the muscles, opening the throat.

(b) In all speech, except when making "m," "n," or "ng" sounds, your throat should be open. Try to keep the sensation of the open throat when you're speaking. The open throat is the way the throat feels after you have yawned and let out your breath.

(c) Follow the exercises for releasing the jaw under mumbling below.

2. Stridency

Follow the exercises for nasality, mumbling, and projection.

3. Lack of projection

Projection is not shouting. Your voice should carry 15 feet (even in a crowded room) without strain. But your backup muscles must be working.

Do the following exercises five minutes at a time, four or five times a day. Do the exercises standing with your shoulders relaxed, the middle of your body vital. Release the tension in the knees. Do not take deep breaths.

(a) Take a breath. Exhale slowly, hissing in a fine stream through your teeth. Mentally count to see how long you can make the hissing last. You should be able to get to 30 the first time and to 70 later on. Pause. Yawn. Do it again.

(b) See how far you can count aloud on a long, single exhalation. Let the numbers come on right after the other, no pause in between. Don't force the process. Stop. Yawn. Do it again.

(c) When you're walking see how far you can go on a single, slow exhalation. A third of a block? A half?

Do the following exercises on the floor.

(a) On your back, knees bent, the back of the next "long" so the chin is not poking up, push the small of the back to the floor. Place your hands on the lower abdomen. Let the shoulders and arms relax. Take in your breath, filling the lower part of the abdomen so you can feel the movement against your hands. Your chest and shoulders should be relaxed and your breathing centered. Let the breath out, through rounded lips. Pause. Repeat.

(b) In the same position, fill "your hands with your breath," hold to a count of five, exhale with your teeth against your bottom lip . . . "fffffff."

Constant, long, slow exhalation is beneficial for air or sea sickness and decreases nervousness.

4. **Unsupported breath (fading)**

Do the exercises for projection. You want to build your breath support by centering your breathing (diaphragm breath control).

5. **Mumbling**

You must get rid of the tension in your jaw, open your mouth more, and make your tongue and lips work for you. Do these exercises:

(a) Looking in the mirror, say a few lines of any verse you memorized as a child. Observe how wide your mouth opens. Say it again, opening the mouth twice as wide as before. Don't tighten the jaw. Keep it relaxed.

(b) Say the word "jaw" five times. Drop the jaw lower with each word.

(c) Say the following words giving each sound its full due: administration, dependability, beautiful, government, exuberance, hereditary, kleptomaniac.

(d) Say the following tongue twisters, slowly. Increase the speed but keep every sound clear:
- The wire is wound around the wheel.
- Around the rugged rock the ragged rascal ran.
- Tessie, the dainty tassel twirled toiled until twilight.

- Red leather, yellow leather.

6. Tension in the jaws	Follow the exercises for mumbling.
7. Hoarseness	Unsupported breath and poor projection can result in hoarseness. Follow the exercises for lack of projection. Cigarette smoke, either yours or someone else's, can cause irritation to the vocal chords making them hoarse:
	Depression can cause the voice to "fall back" into the throat. You just don't have enough energy to project the sound. If hoarseness is a persistent problem, if you are constantly trying to clear your throat, if your voice changes and becomes raspy . . . see your doctor.
8. Monotony of pitch	If your voice is high pitched, do the relaxation exercises we have outlined to do before making a speech or presentation. Tension will cause the voice to be high pitched. Speak more slowly. A rapid rate makes a voice high pitched. Always think "low and slow" before you start to speak. (Don't push your chin down in order to get a lower sound.)
	For more variety in your voice read aloud to small children. Make the story come to life. Hear the variety in the voice.
	Carry the enthusiasm you heard when reading aloud to children over into your every day speech and into speaking situations. Think positively and care about what you're saying and your listeners. By doing this you'll have more color and variety in your voice.

58

9. Rate

Here's where you'll need help — someone who will listen to you and tell you when you're speaking too slowly or too fast. The right rate will seem very slow to you if you have been a "machine gun" speaker or it will be terribly fast if you've been "slow as molasses." Have faith in your monitor and make a habit of speaking at a rate that is comfortable to the ears of your listeners. Practice by reading aloud into a tape machine and playing it back. Check yourself periodically by recording yourself in conversation, when you're making a speech or presentation.

10. Speech mustaches

Tape yourself in conversation or when making a speech or presentation. Listen carefully for the "mustaches" — the "you knows," the "ums" and "ahs."

Consciously correct yourself when you hear yourself making the sounds or adding the unnecessary phrases.

Ask someone you know, who will not nag, to give you a signal every time you make the sound or phrase. (They may just raise a finger.) Rely on them for a short time, then take over the correction yourself, remembering that getting rid of a bad habit takes time.

11. Dialects and accents

Identification of substituted sounds ("d" for the "th," etc.) and distorted vowel sounds and their correction may have to be made by a dialect therapist or speech teacher. (Canadian teachers have diplomas from Mount Royal College and the Toronto Conservatory. American teachers will have studied voice development at recognized universities in the United States. British teachers will hold diplomas from Trinity College of Music, London. International teachers may have diplomas from Canada, the U.S., and England.)

English poetry of the Romantic Period is particularly good for getting the rhythm of spoken English. Read aloud.

Once you have identified the sounds you wish to correct you have to work at least 25 minutes a day on those particular sounds. Then you must consciously correct yourself during conversation. Once again you're changing habits and it takes time.

TALKING BETWEEN THE LINES
(The Metamessage)
Your rate, volume, pitch, and rhythm can send a message to your audience that contradicts what you're saying.

1. Rate	Talking quickly will grab your listener's attention. But in a one-on-one situation it can be construed as coming on too strong. A large audience will soon tune you out if they have to make an effort to keep up with you.
2. Pauses	Pauses between words send signals. The longer the pause, the deeper the feeling you express. Too long — you appear pompous.
3. Volume	Speaking loudly in a small group situation shows excitement and gets attention. But it can also be an attempt to dominate and will put listeners on the defensive.
4. Pitch	When you're angry, afraid or joyous, your vocal cords tense up and shorten.

Your voice gets higher. When you're depressed or tired, your vocal cords sag and lengthen. Your voice drops. Listeners are very aware, unconsciously, of pitch change. Even if you SAY you are not angry or discouraged, they will sense it.

5. Rhythm Smooth speech rhythm shows self-assurance. If your rhythm is broken because you're thinking of grappling with words, it can indicate earnestness. A too slow rhythm can be construed as uncertainty or awkwardness.

6. Disclaimers A laugh, giggle or phrase such as "I think" or "I guess" at the end of a statement indicates you're unsure of yourself.

7. Tag questions Like disclaimers, questions tagged on to statements indicate you're unsure of yourself. They ask for the other person's or the audience's approval. They reflect your lack of confidence, e.g., "The service is terrible, isn't it?"

7
WHAT IS YOUR BODY
SAYING ABOUT YOU?

If your voice presents the message, your body presents the subtext. Some will argue that body language is 95% of the message. We don't advocate anyone becoming an amateur psychologist. Instead we present some of our beliefs based on our experience.

SOLO PERFORMANCES
A vital voice comes from a vital body. If you have a flaccid, tired, apologetic body, you negate your message.

- Beware of the "fig leaf" position. Standing with your hands held crotch level, back of the hands out to the audience presents the weakest image possible.
- Beware of the "reverse fig leaf" position. Holding your hands behind your back a la Prince Phillip is restrictive. From the front you appear to have no arms or hands at all. When you want to gesture, you find yourself merely moving your shoulders like a chicken wanting to fly.
- Don't cross your legs at the ankles and rock back and forth. The image is of an unsure foundation. The audience is not interested in what you have to say; they're interested in when you're going to fall over.

- Crossing your arms across the chest, putting your hands on your hips, and pacing up and down in front of the audience gives them the feeling they're being interrogated. (We've found these to be favorite positions of the police and the military.)

- Jingling coins and keys in your pocket telegraphs to the audience that you're nervous. You should be using that energy in communicating your message. If this is your problem, dump everything out of your pockets before you speak.

- Don't shove your hands deep into your pockets, especially if your pants are of a form fitting design. You'll trap yourself and your gestures will not get made or will appear slightly questionable.

- You present a positive assured image when you stand before an audience with your weight well-balanced on both feet. As much as possible keep your arms and hands free for gestures. Putting a hand in a pocket, thumbs under the belt or holding a lapel is fine. A videotaped rehearsal will let you know if any of these stances give you an arrogant image.

- You present a confident seated image if you keep the spine straight, the shoulders relaxed, and the chest open. Keep your chin parallel to the floor and your arms apart. Don't touch your face or fiddle with your hands or any objects.

PANELS, GROUP PRESENTATIONS, AND NEWS CONFERENCES

When you are on a panel, you're on view even when not speaking. While the camera may select for audience viewing on video or film, it's the audience that selects what they want to look at during a live presentation. Through your body positions and facial expressions, you can either support or contradict what the speaker is saying. Politicians are very aware of how they may "editorialize" as the opposition is speaking. A shrug, a silent laugh, a look of disdain, surprise or boredom can be more powerful than the spoken word. Even the disdainful, sarcastic way you blow cigarette smoke has more to say than words.

When appearing with a group before an audience, make sure you have an alert, listening body. You must appear interested in what the speaker is saying even though you've heard it a thousand times. Panel members are like a Greek chorus. They show the audience how they should react to the speaker. Panel members should not talk to one another while someone else is addressing the audience. What can be more important than what the speaker has to say? These points are particularly important if you're all speaking for the same side. Everyone must appear supportive of the person speaking.

YOUR AUDIENCE

Whether you're speaking to one or one hundred you must "read" your audience. Changing facial expressions, body shifts, and restlessness will tell you you're not getting across or are becoming a bore. When speaking to a group, be prepared to change pace, slow down, ask questions. You're better to sum up quickly than to drone on.

- Although the face is capable of hundreds of nuances of expression, it is easier to control than body reaction. A sudden shift in the body will tell you your listener is reacting to what you're saying. If you're a salesperson and the body shift involves crossing the arms and legs and turning toward the door — you've lost your sale.

- Find the person in the audience who leans forward and nods approvingly as you speak. That listener will boost your ego and you'll speak with renewed confidence.

- If someone who appears to have been in agreement starts to frown or shake the head negatively, consider carefully what you've said. You may need to give further explanation. However, do remember that many people have read books on body language. A rival or competitor may seek to unnerve you by sending out negative signals.

- Crossed arms and legs may mean a defensive attitude toward you and your ideas or it could mean the room is cold.

- Scratching or rubbing the nose may mean the listener doubts what you have to say or it could mean an itchy nose.

- Rubbing the neck at the hairline may mean the listener needs reassurance or has a kink in the neck.

- We caution you not to read body language out of context.

- We recommend two books on body language:

  How to Read A Person Like A Book, Gerald I. Nierenberg and Henry H. Calero, Pocket Books, New York.

  Body Language, Julius Fast, Pocket Books, New York.

8

PACKAGING THE PRESENTER

When you stand before an audience to make a speech or presentation, you may be representing your department, your organization or business. What the audience sees and hears is their impression of, not just you, but what you represent.

Much has been said about dressing for success. So much that there has been a backlash. We do not believe in uniforms. We do not believe that your clothes and grooming will assure success. We believe that success in anything, including making speeches and presentations, comes from attitude, aptitude, and application. However, we do believe that dress, decorum, and good grooming show your respect for yourself, your work, and your audience. We don't believe that you should be packaged into something that you aren't, but cleanliness, pressing, and shining should be everyday habits.

You should not be uncomfortable or present an image that is not you, but you should present the best you possible. The guidelines for dress outlined later in chapter 13 can be followed at all times.

Here are some more:

BASIC CONSIDERATIONS
FOR MEN AND WOMEN

- Consider the clothes rack first: your body. View it nude in front of the mirror from all angles. Consider weight, balance, and posture. Are changes necessary? Can they be done? Will you make them or should you deal realistically with what you see?

- Try on your clothes. View in the mirror for proper fit. If you've gained weight, stretched, pulled fabric gives the impression of neglect and poor grooming. No amount of "sucking in" before the mirror will change that impression. Too big clothes give you a waif-like, lost appearance. Either get your clothes let out or taken in or get rid of them.

- Check lapels and pant legs for extremes of cut. If they are too wide they can be remodelled. Too narrow can't be easily changed. Never buy extremes in fashion for your basic wardrobe. The material will last far longer than the style. Save the unusual for private life.

- Analyze your work and your wardrobe. Separate your work wardrobe from your leisure wardrobe. Does your work wardrobe present a confident, well-groomed image? Are the clothes suitable for the type of work you do? Have you clothes that will take you from your work to the board room to the platform in front of an audience?

- Never buy a new outfit to wear to make a presentation or speech. If the appropriate outfit is not in your wardrobe, buy it well in advance, wear it at appropriate times until it feels comfortable, then wear it to speak.

- Check your existing wardrobe for large, bold patterns, checks, florals and geometrics. This check should include ties. You may be perceived as flamboyant and too daring for your position.

- Similarly check color. This is very important for men. Suits in bright green, electric or baby blue give the audience the impression of the carney or used car salesperson. Women's suits in baby pink or blue can be construed as babyish.

- Polyester fabrics made the iron virtually passé, but pure polyester doesn't present a successful image. It is perceived as being cheap in the sense of worth. Natural fabrics cost more and are expensive to maintain, but they do give the impression of worth. Fortunately there are combinations of cotton and synthetics, wool and synthetics, and silk and synthetics that are good-looking and cheaper to care for. Start a replacement campaign and get rid of the pure polyesters.

- Beware of beige. Beige seems like a nice safe shade. But beige can drain the face of color and make you appear ill, mousey, and blank. Men and women with black, grey or white hair should avoid beige.

- Navy blue is not always the answer. Navy blue can be too dark and overpowering for sandy haired or pale blonde men and women. It can make brown haired people appear sallow. They would be much better in a dark brown. Navy blue looks wonderful on persons with black, grey or white hair.

- If you're very thin, avoid very dark colors. They'll make you appear thinner. Vests narrow the torso.

- If you're carrying extra weight or are very tall and broad, you'll find light colors will make you larger.

- Discard unmercifully. Admit a mistake. Sell it or give it away.
- For business buy the best. Buy basics in classic cuts. Fit is very important. Clothes should be proportioned to your body. Don't buy the current fad for business. Keep those for your leisure life.
- You don't need a lot of clothes for business. Choose pieces that can be interchanged. If you keep your basic wardrobe in one color and your accessories in complementary colors, you can build a wardrobe on very few pieces. You can revive and update your wardrobe with new accessories and pieces.
- Invest in time savers: padded hangers, shoe trees, a Wrinkle-away for travel.
- Keep your clothes washed, ironed, cleaned, and pressed. Shine your shoes. Brush suede. Avoid run-down heels.
- Hang your clothes so that outfits are together and easily reached.
- Shop sensibly at sales. Some bargains can be a waste of money.
- Don't buy if you're thinking:
  (a) "This isn't a good color for me. I'll wear it when I'm feeling good."
  (b) "I have to stand straight/and/ or pull in my stomach to wear this." (We all relax away from the mirror.)
  (c) "I don't know where I'll be able to wear it."
  (d) "It's a little too dressy (or a little too casual) for the office."
- Don't buy it if:
  (a) It's too tight, too short, too big,

not a style you're comfortable in.

    (b) You've gained or lost weight very recently. Wait until you're sure you're stabilized.

- Don't buy:

    (a) Very fragile fabrics for work.

    (b) Very light colors for work. This is particularly true of fabrics that need dry cleaning or special care like light colored suedes and leathers.

    (c) Light colored shoes and boots if you live where you have to walk through rain and salted slush.

- If you hate to shop, find a store and a salesperson who understands you and your work. Let him or her preselect for you. Make an appointment and spend two hours there twice a year. They'll know what you have in your existing wardrobe and you can add to it.

- If you have a poor eye for color, are color blind or feel you've been choosing the wrong colors to suit your natural coloring, have your "colors done" by a color consultant. You'll be given a color book with swatches of the right colors for you which makes choosing clothes easier.

- We emphasize smiling. Smiles draw attention to your teeth. Take care of them.

- Half-glasses add 10 years. Heavy frames take attention away from the eyes. Invest in bifocals with clear glass on top with the correction at the bottom and light frames.

WHAT TO WEAR WHEN MAKING A
SPEECH OR PRESENTATION

- Always check the background of the room or space you'll be speaking in. Choose a color that contrasts with the background so you don't literally fade into the wallpaper. Light shade for dark background, dark for a light background.

- If you're the luncheon or after dinner speaker and your topic is light and entertaining, your clothes can reflect the mood.

- If you're making a speech or presentation to your peers or colleagues, dress and grooming should reflect your own self-esteem, your attitude toward your presentation, and your subject.

- When making presentations to persons in positions higher than yours, you don't have to emulate them in dress but choose the best of your business clothes and present a clean, well-groomed appearance.

- When speaking to persons in positions under you, dress the way you do every day. Don't try a shirt-sleeves approach if that's not you and would be perceived as phoney and contrived. If you have to go out into the field or to smaller towns, don't feel you must dress the same way as your audience. Their work-boots and jeans may be very necessary for the particular work they are doing. You may choose to wear a sports jacket, blazer, corduroy or pants suit that is slightly more casual than your usual business image and that of your position. Pinstripe suits, white shirts, and sincere ties give too much of a boardroom image for the field.

- If you come in from the field to the head office or from a smaller town to the city, choose those clothes that you're comfortable in yet show you have respect for your work. If the last time you wore your suit was to a wedding 10 years ago and it's too small and outdated, don't wear it. You're far better in sports jacket and slacks. Attention to good grooming, from clean nails and hair to polished shoes, is very important. No one likes to be perceived as a rube.

1. Special considerations for women

- Suits aren't the only answer to business dressing. Skirts and smartly coordinated tops or dresses and jackets can provide the same image.
- Don't keep a sweater in your office to wear on cold days. It won't go with everything and will develop bumps and droops.
- Don't burden yourself with briefcase, purse and umbrella. Put them all in one. Briefcases with side pockets will hold an envelope purse and collapsing umbrella.
- Consult a skin and makeup expert. Caring for the skin is essential. Makeup enhances your good features and plays down others. Get into a skin care routine and maintain it. Keep your makeup discreet. Check it for dating — '60's eyes and lips.
- Get a hairstyle that is easy to care for, flattering, and businesslike —

reflecting the way you feel about yourself and your job. It should reveal your face and eyes. Have confidence in your stylist. Don't let your hairstyle date you. Greying or grey hair doesn't have to be dyed. It can be very flattering if it is alive and lifts the face. Long, straight hair on mature women can pull the face down and age it.

- Your eyes and face communicate. Wear flattering accent colors at the neckline directing attention upward.
- Dress and suit hems should not show below a coat unless it is three-quarter length.
- Underwear should be invisible: no bikini lines, bra wrinkles, bunchy slips or saggy straps.
- Pantyhose should fit up to the waist not around the hips. There should be no wrinkles at the ankles. When you've chosen your basic wardrobe colors, find a make that fits in a suitable shade and stock up. When in doubt wear neutral colored hose. Patterned hose is not businesslike.
- Jewelry should be discreet and real.
- Ankle strap shoes are not for business. (They also chop up the long look of the leg and thicken ankles.)
- Choose business shoes with a medium heel height.
- Correcting figure faults with careful dressing:
  (a) Hippy? Stay away from pleats.
  (b) Short-waisted or thick-waisted? Don't define the natural waistline.

(c) Short neck? Avoid large collars.
(d) Heavy legs and feet? Minimize by wearing shoes and hose in the same tones as your outfit.
(e) Short? Choose your blouse and skirt in the same color for a taller, slimmer look.

- Save plunging necklines, excessive frills and ruffles, peek-throughs, and see-throughs for your private life.

- Jogging, hiking, and other athletic wear should be saved for the sports intended.

2. Special considerations for men

- Suits may be your basic wardrobe. But well-styled jackets and pants should not be overlooked. Make sure your basic suit colors are flattering to you. Don't choose to wear navy because it is "businesslike." You may look much better in brown.

- Short sleeve shirts may be great to work in, but when you're meeting with upper management wear long sleeve shirts. The touch of white or pale color at the cuff is good.

- Don't overburden your pockets. Lumps and bumps look untidy.

- If you have skin problems, see a dermatologist. Skin care is as important to men as it is to women. Warts, moles, and blemishes can be removed.

- Get a barber you like. Don't skip haircuts. The very day you think you can let it go for another week can be the day you want to make a good impression. Wash your hair frequently and keep it groomed.

Unfortunately the dandruff ads are right. People are repelled by it. Beards can be flattering but should always be clean and trimmed.

- White may not be the best color in shirts for you. White can make some skin sallow. You may be better off to choose shirts in very soft shades of your suit color.

- Avoid flamboyant colors and patterns when choosing ties. Don't wear a tie just because someone you love gave it to you as a gift. Ties with narrow stripes with a fine red line are considered sincere and honest by the experts. You may use your own discretion.

- Buy coats large enough to fit comfortably over a suit. You don't want to look as though your coat shrunk or you're drowning inside it.

- Buy shirts with tails long enough to be tucked inside so they don't creep out.

- Fitted shirts are fine but should not appear to have shrunk.

- Pants should fit up around the waist. (We can honestly say we've been half-mooned by several presenters when they bent over.)

- Wear executive length socks. Baggy socks and exposed shanks don't present a businesslike image.

- Double-breasted jackets make you broader. Vests make you narrower. (With the accent on fitness and good health, paunches do not present a good business image.)

- Jewelry should be discreet and real. Gold bracelets and neck chains have never been an accepted business image.

- Your shoes should complement your outfit. Wingtip oxfords, other tie shoes, loafers and pumps all have their place. Save the leisure shoes and running shoes for leisure and sports.
- White belts and white shoes do not present a good business image.
- Save the white socks, the tweed jackets with leather trim and tabs, the hiking boots, the jogging and athletic wear for your private life.

9

CONFIDENCE AND SELF-CONTROL

Being nervous about speaking is natural. Like an athlete who is up for the game, you're feeling the flow of adrenalin. If you're prepared and well-rehearsed, you can turn that nervousness into energy. (If you're not prepared and well-rehearsed, you have every right to be nervous.)

You need a certain amount of anxiety and tension in order to perform well. Unfortunately, many speakers start to focus on their anxiety rather than on the business of communicating their message. They compound the problem by telegraphing their anxiety to the audience or openly asking for sympathy. Instead, use that energy to reach your audience. Develop the attitude that the energy is normal and beneficial. It will improve your powers of concentration and communication.

If you develop cold, sweaty hands before speaking, use that as a signal that you're ready to speak. No one is going to be holding your hands so no one but you will know they're cold and sweaty. Here are some things you can control.

CONTROLLING SIGNS OF NERVOUSNESS

1. Dry mouth   If your mouth becomes dry, drop your head thoughtfully during a natural pause and bite the side of your tongue (gently!). This causes the saliva to flow. Have a glass of water handy. Take a small sip during a natural pause. (Don't take a large gulp. You could choke.) Do not use lifesavers or mints. They interfere with articulation and you could inadvertently swallow one and choke.

2. Too much saliva

If you mouth fills with saliva and you feel you're spraying the first four rows, put the tip of your tongue on the hard ridge behind the top teeth (the position for making "t" and "d"). Open your mouth and breath in through the mouth. This position allows the air to dry the saliva without drying the tongue and vocal cords.

3. Drying up

If you dry up or lose your train of thought, take your eye contact away from the audience. Take a deep breath. Let it out slowly as you look down at your notes and collect your thoughts. Focus on what you are saying, not that you are drying. You may repeat part of what you've said to help you and your audience get back on track. Be very natural and conversational. The time it takes to do this may seem horrendously long to you but, in truth, it will be a matter of seconds.

4. Tight throat

Learn to yawn secretly. We all did it in school. Drop the head, keep the lips together, open the back of the throat and pull the air in through the nose. This is the best exercise to release tension than can build in the throat. When you feel your throat tightening, don't take a sip of water. The swallow can increase the tension. Instead, yawn secretly and open the throat.

5. Shaking

Shaking hands and trembling knees are not fear. It's the homeostatic process of the body dissipating excess energy. Don't try to control this process by clutching the lectern or shoving your hands in your pockets. You're just adding to the problem. Use this excessive energy positively. Make motivated gestures and body movement. Gestures must be motivated by what you're saying. Let them happen naturally and fully. Restrained, nervous little flicks send out the message — nervous. Large gestures are signs of confidence. Bodily movement must also be motivated to bring you closer to the audience, to fill a pause with meaning or to emphasize a point. Random pacing or nervous repeated gestures can destroy a speech. Motivated gestures and body movement support and aid effective communication.

6. Shortness of breath If you become short of breath or can't get your breath when speaking, stop talking. Drop your head and take your focus from your audience. Cross your left arm across the lowest part of your abdomen. Relax the shoulders. Take a deep breath into the lowest part of your abdomen. You should feel the pressure of your abdomen pushing against your crossed arm. Let the breath out slowly through your lips. Take in your next breath the same way while lifting your head and start to speak. This is a condensed version of deep breathing and sighing which relaxes you and centers your breath.

7. Butterflies You can get rid of the butterflies by tensing the muscles of the buttocks and abdomen. Hold. Relax. (One of our clients has used this exercise to improve his putting.)

8. Facial tension Smile! Not only will it relax you, it will also relax your audience.

79

RELAXATION EXERCISES

These are exercises you can do in your office or the ante-room before you speak. A few you can do right at a conference table and no one will be the wiser.

1. Breath

- Centered breath is essential. Take in a deep breath low into the body and let it out slowly with a sigh. The sigh relaxes you. Yawn and let the breath out with a long sigh.

2. Face

- Smile broadly saying "eeeh." Tighten the area below your jowls so you feel bulges on either side of the front of the neck. Purse your lips strongly and say "oooh." Repeat 10 times.
- Screw your face all into the middle. Hold. Relax. Open eyes and mouth as wide as you can. Hold. Relax.
- Pinch your eyebrows between thumbs and forefingers. Hold. Release.

3. Jaw

- Tilt your head back slightly, supporting it at the back with your hands. Push lower jaw out and up until you feel tension in chin and throat. Make 20 little upward thrusts with your jaw. Relax. Repeat three times.
- Drop the jaw. Repeat the word jaw pushing the mouth open wider with each repetition. Repeat 10 times.

4. Neck

- Sit up straight. Tilt head to one side as if you were trying to touch your ear to your shoulder. Don't lift shoulder to ear. Hold for count of five. Repeat on the other side.

Repeat entire exercise four times.

- Facing forward, turn head to one side as far as possible, as if trying to look behind you. Hold for a count of five. Repeat on the other side. Repeat entire exercise four times.

- Keeping shoulders still, rotate head in a wide semicircle to the right, then forward and down, then up to the left. Don't do a complete circle. Rolling the head back may do damage to the spine.

5. Shoulders and arms

- Cross the right arm over the chest and grasp the shoulder muscle. Hold. Circle the left arm backwards three times. Push the arm straight down to a count of five. Release your hold. Repeat the exercise with the left arm holding the muscle of the right shoulder.

- Sit up straight. Raise shoulders as high as possible. Hold for a count of five. Lower shoulders as far as possible. Hold for five count. Repeat three times.

- Sit up straight. Roll one shoulder forward in a wide circular motion making three complete circles. Repeat rolling backwards. Repeat entire exercise with the other shoulder, then with both shoulders simultaneously.

- Reach right arm over left shoulder to touch shoulder blade. Hold for a five count. Repeat with left arm. Relax. Repeat.

- Clench fists tightly. Let the tension go up the arm into the jaw. Hold. Relax. Shake out the arm. Let the jaw drop.

81

6. Upper body

- With elbows out to the sides, clasp hands at chest height by hooking fingers. Pull back as if trying to break your own fingerhold. Hold for a count of five. Relax. Repeat.

- Stretch arms out in front of you, fingers locked. Push outward with upper arms and shoulders as if trying to force your shoulder blades apart. Tuck head to get a good stretch. Hold for five count. Relax. Repeat.

7. Legs and feet

- Curl toes. Hold. Relax.

- Place hands on outsides of knees and press inward. At the same time try to force knees apart. Keep up the resistance to a count of five. Relax. Repeat.

- Cross right leg over left. Stretch right foot, pointing toe down as far as possible. Relax. Repeat eight times. Then repeat with left foot.

10

TODAY'S THE DAY: GIVING YOUR SPEECH OR PRESENTATION

Because you're prepared and well-rehearsed, you're ready to make your speech or presentation. You know how to turn your nerves into energy, which will give you the edge in making a successful performance. To give you additional assurance use this check list.

CHECKLIST PRIOR TO SPEECH OR PRESENTATION

(a) Check your notes or script. Are they in proper order? Secure them together, but don't staple them. You'll just have to take the staples out. Rubber bands work for cards. Large paper clips work for both cards and pages.

(b) Put your notes into your pocket, purse or briefcase. If possible, have a duplicate set very close by. When traveling, keep notes on your person. Take your slides with you on the plane. If you don't, you won't be the first speaker who arrived in Toronto while the notes and visual aids got off in New York.

(c) Recheck all audio-visual material to assure it is in order.

(d) Check to see you have additional bulbs, extension cords, etc.

(e) Take your security blanket (aspirins, handkerchief, extra pantyhose, glasses, extra glasses). Remember Murphy's Law.

(f) Check the news. Does it affect or influence your speech or presentation? Be ready to incorporate or change.

(g) If you are making an in-house presentation, take a pulse reading of your company. Very recent decisions could affect your presentation. Be aware of what is going on.

(h) Check to see that there have been no last minute changes in the program or agenda.

(i) If you're making your presentation with someone else, allow time to meet and make final reassurances.

(j) Arrive early.

(k) Check the set-up of the room. Rearrange if necessary.

(l) Test the microphone, if you'll be using one.

(m) Set up audio-visual material.

(n) Check to make sure equipment is working.

(o) If using slides, run through quickly as a final check that they're in order.

(p) Focus overhead, etc.

(q) Check for distraction. People will read, and re-read any printed matter on the walls. Take down posters. If you speak after someone else, be sure all their visuals have been removed before you speak.

(r) Make a final visit to the washroom. Make sure your hair is well-groomed at the back as well as the front. If you speak after a meal, check and if possible brush your teeth. Shelley Berman isn't the only one who has discovered, too late, that there was spinach between his teeth.

Tuck in shirt tails all around, button all buttons, and zipper all zippers. (Refrain from rechecking your zipper when you are going up to speak or in front of an audience.)

(s) If you need water at the lectern, check to see that it is there. Don't rely on someone else to get it.

OUR FINAL WORD BEFORE YOU SPEAK

Like any coach before the big game, we want to give you some last words of encouragement and advice before you speak.

- Eat lightly. No matter what time of day you speak you want your blood focused on your brain not your digestion.
- Don't drink alcohol. It will give you false courage, impaired articulation, and scrambled ideas.
- Don't drink milk. It makes mucous.
- Don't drink carbonated beverages. Stifling a burp can undermine confidence.
- If you are at a head table, remember you are "on" before you speak. The audience is looking at you in anticipation.
- Keep your body alert.
- Don't cross your legs. It stops circulation.
- If you're being introduced, listen. You must acknowledge.

- When you get up to speak, walk with purpose and confidence.

- Take your time before you begin to speak. Take a 1-2-3 count. Look out at your audience. Smile. Establish your presence. Get your breathing centered.

- Remain flexible. You might need to update your speech or presentation. The unexpected *can* happen.

- Remember: there is the speech you are going to give; the one you give; and the one you wish you'd given. When you're well-organized and well-rehearsed, they are more likely to be the same speech. Learn from the differences; apply that knowledge to the next time you speak.

NOW ARE THERE ANY QUESTIONS?

The moment you say those words you have lost control of the situation and given it to the audience. Each time you answer a question you have to regain control. Too often speakers say, "Oh, I have nothing prepared. I'll just let the audience ask questions." Those speakers are expecting the audience to do their work for them. Other speakers use, "Are there any questions?" as a conclusion to their speeches or presentations. They seek an easy way out and fail to use their conclusions to make their points strong and memorable.

Your speech or presentation should include most of the answers to anticipated questions. If it doesn't, your audience will become frustrated and concentrate on the unanswered questions, not listening to your full presentation. Or you can become overwhelmed by questions at the end. Some listeners will become too frustrated and angry to ask questions at all. They have reached a conclusion.

You may not wish to answer a question in complete detail during your presentation. But be armed to answer in detail during the question period in case someone in the audience wants details. Don't leave something important out of your speech or presentation because you think a member of the audience will ask the question that will allow you to expand and appear knowledgeable. Quite often that question may never be asked. If you feel it is significant, make the point within your presentation.

1. Asking for questions during a presentation	We reiterate. Every time you open for questions you lose the ball to the other court. There is also a loss of continuity. You add an additional burden to get yourself, your audience, and your presentation back on track. "Now where were we?" Only open for questions during a presentation if your material is technical or complex and, by reading your audience, you sense their confusion. We believe that careful organization and use of appropriate visuals will assure a firm grasp of the facts and eliminate the need for questions.
2. Kinds of questions	(a) *Neutral questions* usually request information or clarification.
	(b) *Friendly questions* betray a bias toward what you have said, e.g., "I agree with what you say, but want can we do . . .?
	(c) *Antagonistic or hostile questions* are usually prefaced with argument or disagreement with what you have said, e.g. "Do you mean to tell me . . .?" In business antagonistic questions can arise because of company politics, rivalry, resentment, status-seeking, and competition. That's why we stress analyzing your audience carefully before you plan your presentation so you're aware of who will be there.

3. Answering questions

- Never assume a superior air. State your case moderately and accurately. If you treat a questioner with arrogance, you're likely to turn the whole audience against you.

- Answer neutral and friendly questions by giving information.

- Satisfy hostile questions that you understand why they feel the way they do, that you don't feel hostile toward them personally, and that you want to establish common ground with them. Preface your answer, e.g., "I know it's difficult to accept the facts, but the evidence is there. Let me repeat it for you."

- Listen carefully to the question.

- Repeat or paraphrase the question so you are sure you understand it and so everyone in the audience hears it.

- Define terms, either from the question or terms you'll be using.

- If necessary, divide the question into several parts, and deal with each part separately.

- Always tell the truth.

- Be brief and to the point. Limit your answer to the question. Do not introduce something new.

- If a questioner interrupts: pause and let him finish, then continue with your answer. Don't try to talk louder. Don't let him get you off the point of your answer. If he persists in interrupting, don't get into an argument. Try to complete your answer. Your audience will recognize his rudeness and take your side.

- If you have answered a questioner, but she keeps going over and over the question, ask the audience if you have answered fully enough. If they assure you you have, then move on to the next question.
- Deal with each question one at a time. If a questioner asks several questions in one, ask what the main question is and deal with that or deal with the one you are most comfortable with.
- If a question contains untrue information, e.g., "Your company is laying off staff," correct the fact, then deal with the question. Once you have dealt with the erroneous material there may be no question.
- Relate your answers to your speech or presentation, e.g., "As I said . . . ."
- If a question is strongly argumentative, answer it directly, maintaining your point of view.
- Don't let a questioner give a speech. Cut in and ask what the question is.
- If someone has difficulty wording a question, assist.
- Avoid jargon, departmental language, and abbreviations.
- Don't let others put words into your mouth or try to read your thoughts, e.g., "Then you believe . . . ." Restate what you are saying. State it clearly.
- Don't be afraid to say, "I don't know." Then go on to say you'll get the information or tell them where the information is available.
- Don't make rash promises.

- Don't allow one or two people to monopolize the question period.

4. Handling a heckler

- Pause. Don't try to talk over the heckler's voice.
- Acknowledge.
- Offer to talk with the heckler later.
- Invite the heckler to come and speak.
- Let the audience assume responsibility for quieting the heckler.
- Do not argue.
- Remain rational, objective, and nonretaliatory.
- Be prepared to receive wounds without showing they have been inflicted.
- Never lose your temper.

11

IT'S NOT A BEDTIME STORY — DON'T PUT US TO SLEEP

There are times when a text must be read, but this method has pitfalls. Reading a speech, presentation text or technical paper is more difficult than delivering an extemporaneous speech. It requires more practice and preparation for these reasons:

(a) Voices lose animation and vitality when you read.

(b) If you read without practice, you lose eye contact with your audience.

(c) When you read without rehearsal, you tend to speed your rate resulting in poor articulation and lost sounds.

(d) Reading without rehearsal results in less projection.

PREPARATION FOR SCRIPT READING

- The paper should have a stiffness to it.
- Use large type. Speech or orator types are available for most typewriters. You may prefer to use upper and lower case letters rather than the upper case of the orator type. However, for the sake of larger print, you can train yourself to read upper case type.
- Center the type on the page keeping the lines four to five inches in

length. This allows the eye to pick up bites of type easily. (See the example on page 93.)

- Use periods, three or more, or dashes instead of commas. This makes you pause naturally as you read. You can use the same method to set a word apart to give it vocal emphasis.

- The script should be double or triple spaced. We double space a sentence; triple space between sentences and use four spaces between paragraphs.

- Start each new sentence at the right margin.

- Start each main point at the top of a page. You may have to leave the preceding page three quarters blank. There is a lift and new energy to the voice when starting a new page. This is important when you want to get a new point across.

- A paragraph should end on a page. Sentences should be completed on a page. You don't want to turn the page in the middle of a thought.

- If you're a rapid reader or tend to drop your head, type the text on only two thirds of the page. Never let type fall below the three-quarters point of the page.

- Use only one side of the paper.

- Number the pages. We prefer the number in the right-hand corner.

- Don't staple pages. If they're stapled, take the staple out.

- As you speak, you're going to move the pages to one side when they are completed. You may wish to turn

SAMPLE PAGE OF A SCRIPT

LET'S TALK ABOUT MONEY.

IN TODAY'S ECONOMIC CRISIS . . . WE CAN RIGHTLY ASK . . .
WHAT HAS HAPPENED TO MONEY?

EIGHT YEARS AGO . . YOU HAD MONEY IN YOUR POCKET . .
MONEY IN YOUR BANK.
YOU SPENT BECAUSE YOU KNEW YOUR WAGES WOULD
INCREASE ACCORDINGLY.
IF YOU DIDN'T HAVE THE CASH IN YOUR POCKET . . .
YOU CHARGED WHAT YOU WANTED.
YOUR CREDIT CARDS REPRESENTED MONEY.

IF YOU DIDN'T HAVE ENOUGH MONEY . . . YOU COULD
BORROW MORE.

MONEY FLOWED EASILY.

THEN . . . SUDDENLY . . . THE FLOW STOPPED . . .
MONEY DISAPPEARED.

up a corner at the top or bottom so you can grasp the page to slide it across. (Hold with one hand, slide with the other.)

- You may mark the script where you wish to give greater emphasis, slow down or pause. Don't over-mark. Cute pictures and multi-colors can cause confusion rather than create clarity. (Have a rehearsal script and a final one for presentation. Transfer markings that are absolutely necessary for performance. Be sure to rehearse with presentation script.)

- Have a podium for your script. If the podium is too deep and your head has to drop down to read the script, use a block of wood nine inches long, four inches wide, and an inch deep. Place it on the lip of the podium. It will push your script higher for better eye contact. If you have to give speeches or make presentations where you're not sure of the facilities, you may want to invest in a portable podium.

- Be sure you can be seen from behind the podium. Build a box to stand on if necessary. Talking eyebrows are amusing but when the text is being read, you must assure that the audience sees you.

- The script you prepare to read from is not the script that is given to the press, or printed. That text is set out on the page in the usual manner.

- You may find in rehearsal that some sentences are too long, some phrases cumbersome, some words present pronunciation problems. Change them to make it easier for you. The text that goes to the press, public or printer need not be changed if the sense and intent remain the same.

- Never hand out a text in advance of delivery. Your audience is not there to test your oral reading ability. The only exception is if the press must meet a deadline.

- On occasion we have had clients put their text or script into a loose-leaf binder. This keeps the pages together. However, the turning of the page is obvious to the audience and can be distracting if not done with ease.

- You may feel that you have too large a stack of paper when you set it out as we advise. You'll find, however, that the assistance it gives you far outweighs the bulk. (Your audience is also pleasantly surprised to find that the stack of paper did not mean a long speech.)

CLEAR WRITING FOR CLEAR SPEAKING

- Use the active voice. Make the actor the subject whenever possible.
- Write sentences averaging less than 20 words.
- Use a variety of sentence lengths so one long sentence doesn't follow another.
- Keep subject, verb, and object or complement close together. Avoid suspended sentences where the completion of thought is suspended until you get to the verb and its complement.
- Translate jargon and special vocabulary for general audiences. Jargon is elitist. It fails to communicate clearly even within a field.
- Don't use acronyms.
- Be specific. Get rid of vague and meaningless modifiers: appreciably, excessive, fairly, nearly, negligible, rather, reasonably, relatively, significant, somewhat, substantial, sufficient, suitable, undue, various.

- Get rid of pretentious phrases. John Dean of Watergate fame gave the world "at this point in time." We don't need it. Nor do we need: at the present time, currently or presently (which means soon). Use now!

- Clear away the deadwood: as a matter of fact, to be honest (haven't you been up to now?), I might add, it is interesting to note, it should be pointed out, it should be remembered, it is worthy to say, for your information, may I say, may I call your attention, may I take the liberty, permit me to say, with your kind permission.

- Eliminate the indefinite "this" at the beginning of a sentence. Make antecedents clear.

- Simplify verb tenses. Keep to the simple present (he goes), simple past, (he went) and simple future (he will go). Avoid compound tenses (she is going, she would have gone).

- Avoid "there is" and "there are", the substitute for the finite verb.

- Use the present tense when citing from a book (Aristotle reminds us, or Dickens puts it another way) except when specifying a time (Winston Churchill stated in 1942).

- Get rid of redundancies. (See Appendix 1.)

- Get rid of cliches and overworked phrases. (See Appendix 2.)

REHEARSAL AND DELIVERY

- If you did not write the text yourself, read it through silently in

96

order to absorb the sense of it.

- After reading it silently, ask yourself what the purpose is. State (aloud) what points and facts remain with you.

- Read silently again and repeat the previous step. This will give you an idea of what you must emphasize when you are reading in order for your audience to retain the same impressions you got from the silent reading.

- Eye contact is extremely important. You must learn to read much as a television reporter reads from a script. Delivering a written text depends on your ability to read, retain, and deliver. For that reason, read only the number of words that are right for you. This may not mean full sentences. How the speech is set out on the page is important for this step.

- Look down at the page; silently read a group of words. Look up and deliver them, making eye contact with the audience and putting full meaning into the words. Keep repeating this. The pace may seem slow to you but it won't be for your audience who is absorbing what you have to say.

- Keeping the head up during delivery is difficult. If you have trouble, just make sure you're looking at your audience as you begin a sentence, and, more importantly, when you finish a sentence. Don't let your head and voice drop at the end of a sentence. It weakens and negates everything that has gone before. Through practice you'll find you can read and deliver greater portions of the text at a time. It takes many sessions of oral practice to make the words lift off the page smoothly and come to life.

- Deliver the text with tremendous enthusiasm and greater projection when you rehearse. Feel the vitality in your voice and body. Overdo. It'll be just right when you actually deliver it.

- Practice at least once with an audience. It may be just one person. Tape it and listen back. Don't tape as if it were a radio presentation. Tape it under the same circumstances as you'll be delivering it. Does it have vitality? Do you sound like you are speaking or reading? You want it to sound like the former.

- When delivering your text use a finger as a marker. If you lose your place when looking up and down don't signal your concern to the audience. Pick up where you left off even if it means repeating a phrase. Give it more emphasis and it will appear to be intentional.

- When you come to the end of your text slow your rate. Deliver the text looking directly at your audience. Your voice should have more strength and intensity. In this way you signal your audience that you're making your final statement.

USING A MICROPHONE

- Check the microphone in advance.

- Have someone help you take a balance.
- Find out if someone is in control of the sound system.
- Practice raising and lowering the microphone if someone is going to speak before you. Don't lean over or look up to speak if someone has left the microphone too low or high.
- Find out how you can turn the sound off. You may want to turn it off if you need to cough or sneeze. (Those things do happen!) But try to avoid making unpleasant sounds over the microphone.
- Lavaliere microphones which clip to your tie or lapel allow you to move your head more when you're speaking and allow for greater freedom of movement and the use of both hands.
- Directional stand microphones do not allow for a great deal of movement. Your mouth should be from eight to twelve inches from the microphone. To look at the audience on the left or right, tilt your head but keep your mouth in line with the microphone. There is nothing more disconcerting than a speaker who turns his or her head from one side to the other, the voice fading in and out.
- Hand-held microphones allow you to move freely and keep your voice projected. You must keep the mike at the same distance from your mouth at all times. You lose the use of one hand and arm for gestures and demonstration.
- Lavaliere and hand-held microphones, other than transistor

mikes, have cords to contend with when you move around.

- Don't say anything confidential near a microphone.
- Don't get so close to a microphone that your "p's" pop and your "s's" hiss. You're not a rock singer.
- Don't think of speaking "to the microphone!" Speak to the people in the first row. Microphones give the voice more volume but they don't give energy. You have to supply the enthusiasm.
- Don't hit a microphone or blow into it to test it. Count into it at the volume you will be using. Because you've arrived early to check it, you can try a few lines or ideas from your speech or presentation.
- Squeals or feedback come from setting the volume too high or having the speakers placed too close to the microphone.
- Once the sound system acts up, you're in trouble. For that reason we cannot overemphasize pre-checking. It also helps for you to develop your voice so you can speak and fill any space without a microphone and not damage the vocal cords.

12

SPEAKING IMPROMPTU UNDER PRESSURE

If you find it difficult to speak in impromptu situations, you must be prepared for them.

TRAINING YOURSELF FOR IMPROMPTU SPEAKING

- Write topic titles on single cards. Place the cards in a box or bowl. Draw one out at random.

- Quickly narrow the topic to what you can speak on. (Don't write anything down. All steps of this exercise should be done mentally.) Consider the audience.

- Think of the main point or points you want to get across.

- Decide on your conclusion. What you want them to know or to do when you're finished speaking. Be very sure of your conclusion. The danger with impromptu speaking is that you don't know when to stop talking. A "few words" can become rambling rhetoric if you don't have a firm conclusion in mind before you start to talk.

- Begin with a strong statement letting the audience know what you're going to talk about.

- This mental preparation follows the same steps we advocate for making speeches or presentations.

Only the time factor is much shorter. Your preparation and opening statement should take no more than 15 seconds. With practice you'll be able to get it down to five.

- Once organized speak aloud. Tape if possible. Did you stay on topic? Did you get across the points of your mental organization? Did you have a strong conclusion?

- Daily practice of this exercise is imperative if you wish to become comfortable and confident speaking impromptu.

MEETINGS

Never go into a meeting without considering that you may have to speak.

- If there is an agenda, study it carefully. Do any of the items concern you? Is there a spin-off from any that could have some relationship to what you're doing?

- Who is attending the meeting? Could any of them have a hidden agenda that could have a bearing on you?

- Even though it doesn't appear on the agenda, review for yourself what you're working on, or what you've just completed, or may be working on in the future. Update yourself on facts and figures.

- When called upon to speak:
  (a) Make sure you understand the question. Paraphrase or ask that it be repeated.
  (b) Take your eyes away from the questioner. Focus on what you want to say. Quickly determine

your main points. Decide on your conclusion.

(c) One of the best formats for an impromptu answer is to have your main points cover past, present, and future.

(d) Support main points with specifics. If you don't have them with you, assure that the information will be sent to all concerned.

(e) Take your time, keep cool.

(f) Avoid rambling, getting off the subject, apologizing, acting surprised, or deprecating yourself.

(g) Come to a strong conclusion and stop talking. (One of our professors said, "Stand up, speak up, shut up." It's good advice. The greatest fault with impromptu speaking is not coming to a conclusion.)

13

LET'S MEET THE MEDIA

More and more business people must answer reporters' questions, be interviewed on the telephone or appear on television. Too often the experience is disastrous for both the person and the company represented. You can make the media work for you rather than against you if you have an understanding of the workings of the media and are well-prepared.

MEDIA DIFFERENCES

1. Radio   Radio is the immediate medium. News can be aired the moment it breaks. You can be live "on air" when reached by telephone. You can be taped and excerpts used both in and out of context.

2. Television   Television is the next most immediate medium. In surveys, it has also been named as the most believed of the news media. Because you are both seen and heard the impression is the strongest.

3. Print   Print is the least immediate. The daily paper is hours behind radio and television in getting the news to the public. However, it can provide greater detail and it is longer lasting. Magazines and books have these same qualities to a greater degree. More and more reporters and feature writers are using tape recorders when getting a story for print. Tapes (unedited) provide protection against misquotes.

RULES FOR GOOD PRESS RELATIONS

Rule one: Nothing is off the record.

Rule two: Reporters do not work for you. Don't tell them what to do or expect them to believe what you're telling them just because you are who you are.

Rule three: Never lie. If you don't know the answer say so. If possible give the name of the person or agency who can give the answer.

Rule four: Never say "no comment." It alienates a television audience and sets the reporter or interviewer on the scent of the real story. Always be prepared with an answer for any question that can be asked. Respond briefly to a negative question and follow quickly with something positive.

Rule five: Don't let a reporter or interviewer put words in your mouth. Correct with charm. "No, that is not what I said (think, feel). I said (think, feel)." "Neither of those is correct. Let me tell you what is."

Rule six: Don't ramble. Keep your answers short and on the subject. Condense your answer to three points. The press wants pithy, substantive quotes 15 to 20 seconds long. Anticipate questions in advance and have your quotes ready.

Rule seven: Know in advance what your story is and get it across no matter what questions you are asked. Tell the good news.

Rule eight: Don't engage in verbal sparring with a reporter.

Rule nine: Never lose your temper with the press.

Rule ten: Don't be afraid of silence. Take your time before you answer. Think about your answer. On radio or television it's the responsibility of the interviewer to fill silence. The interviewer may either elaborate or come up with another question if the pause is too long. In a print interview, silence doesn't have to be filled with sound. Give the reporter time to digest what you have said and formulate the next question. Reporters can't think while you are talking. Never do more than answer the question. You may say more than you intended.

Rule eleven: Company policy statements should be formulated on every important issue so that everyone involved knows what should be revealed to the press.

Rule twelve: Shoot squarely. If the information is confidential, be prepared for the question with an answer that is honest but not evasive.

Rule thirteen: Give service. Keep appointments. Keep promises. Provide information.

Rule fourteen: Be aware of what is happening in any area of your profession. It may not be your oil well that is on fire or your company that is going bankrupt or firing personnel but that doesn't mean you won't get a related question.

WHO ARE THESE MEDIA PEOPLE AND WHAT ARE THEY LOOKING FOR?

- Newspersons consider themselves the watchdogs for the public.
- They are looking for news.
- They are not extensions of your public relations department.
- They want a story that has crises, conflict, and controversy.
- You want to give the newsperson selected information, but the newsperson always has other questions in mind:
  - (a) Who stands to gain?
  - (b) Who stands to lose?
  - (c) Will there be conflict?
  - (d) What are they hiding?
  - (e) Are there political overtones?
  - (f) Is this a small part of something much larger?
  - (g) Are there far-reaching ramifications (international)?
  - (h) Are they trying to protect or cover someone or something?
  - (i) Are relationships as they appear or is there internal conflict?
- Don't use professional jargon and acronyms.
- They are often working on several stories at once and may not have all the information as a background to their questioning or interview with you.

1. What do they want?
- They want information from you that they can't get otherwise.

	• They want you to confirm or refute information they have.
	• They want an opinion or statement that can be directly quotable to you.
2. What will they ask?	• To get information, they'll ask questions beginning with who, what, when, where, and how.
	• To get confirmation or refutation, they'll ask questions that are usually answered with yes or no.
	• To get an opinion or statement, they will ask probing questions beginning most often with why.
3. What else do they look for?	• Reporters look for conflicting messages from what you are saying and what your body language and vocal intonation reveals.
	• Facial expression, nervous movement, vocal pitch change, increase in vocal intensity, and overuse of the upward inflection tell reporters they are getting close to something.
	• Nervous laughter can be interpreted literally by a reporter, i.e., "The president of Patooks Oil laughed as he confirmed that four men had been killed at the drilling site."
	• Reporters look for over-justification and over-confidence. They can get you to disclose more.
	• Reporters look for suppressed anger. If they can provoke you more, they can get you to lose control and reveal more.

THE TELEVISION INTERVIEW

- The interviewer may not be thoroughly prepared, but you must be. Anticipate negative or offbeat questions. Know what you want to get across. Have your facts and figures firmly fixed in your mind. (You may bring notes, but you appear more authoritative without them.)

- You are the expert on your subject. You control the interview.

- Keep your answers direct and to the point. Use stories and analogies to illustrate your points.

- Don't digress. You may bring up questions you're not prepared to answer.

- Don't be too technical. It may be simple to you but it could be complex for the average viewer.

- Defuse highly charged questions by remaining relaxed. Restate the question, eliminating all disparaging words and references.

- If you are representing your company, never give your own opinion if it is in conflict with your company. People remember you as the image of your company.

- Never go on television when you're tired. Tired translates as "bored" on television. This can be particularly bad during a crisis situation.

- Watch a broadcast of the program you'll be appearing on. Familiarize yourself with the format, the interview habits of the interviewer, and the set. (You don't want to fade into the furniture by wearing the wrong clothes.)

- Your credibility will come through your tone of voice, your posture, facial expression, accuracy of information, enthusiasm, and sincerity. Viewers remember general impressions more than specific facts.

See the sample interview in Appendix 3.

1. Your television image

- Wear an outfit that reflects your professional image.
- Avoid loud patterns, herringbone stripes, leather, ultra-suede, shiny or stiff materials.
- Avoid large amounts of black, white, and dark navy blue which photographs black.
- Don't wear large amounts of red or yellow near the face. They tend to bleed into the face.
- The best basic colors for television are pastels, beiges, browns, blues, and greys with accent colors. Light colors give you a more youthful appearance on TV.
- Men should wear knee-high stockings.
- Women should not wear narrow skirts, which tend to ride up.
- Women should avoid excessive or jangly jewelry.
- Lights wash out facial color. Women should wear more of their natural shades of makeup. Blend well and set with powder. Do not

wear colored eye shadow. Wear coral lipstick, not red.

- Men should not refuse makeup. Without it you'll appear washed out. A tan is the best TV makeup for men.
- Keep your hair the width of two fingers above your eyebrows or you'll appear beetle-browed. Spray down hair that sticks up. The camera exaggerates, and an unruly cowlick gives you an ungroomed or rube appearance. If you're balding, let them powder your head and eliminate glare.
- Make a final check before you go on the air. Check zippers. Check your tie. If it is slightly askew it gives you a careless appearance and viewers may feel you approach your subject in the same way.
- Once seated, pull your jacket down in front so it won't horseshoe around your neck.
- Don't slump in the chair. Be alert but not tense. Undo your coat jacket if it's buckling out. But remember that large expanses of white shirt will make you photograph fatter. Vests look good on TV unless you are very thin, then they'll make you appear thinner.
- Don't cross your legs in the four position. It allows for crotch shots, pictures of the bottoms of your shoes, and the temptation to fiddle with your shoelaces.
- If it's a swivel chair, steel yourself against moving. It is extremely distracting for the viewer and sets up a rhythm for you which will affect your delivery.

2. On camera

- Present the person in charge with a card with your name, title, and company name typed on it. Don't use a business card. Use a file card. They should have all this information, but it doesn't hurt to reinforce.

- Look at the interviewer. Don't let your gaze move around. You don't have to worry about the camera. If you have to avert your gaze, look down thoughtfully, but look up again when you speak. If you keep your gaze down when speaking, you'll appear, not humble, but evasive.

- Your microphone will be attached to your lapel. Don't touch it.

- Use conversational tones. Your microphone will be tested before you go on the air for natural projection. Talk to the interviewer with the same vitality you have normally. Vocal vitality is important in getting your message across.

- Let your body, voice, and face show interest and purpose. Lean slightly forward.

- Your smallest gesture will be magnified when you are on camera. Don't be afraid to use gestures, just move more slowly so the camera can keep you in the picture. Keep gestures above the waist in camera view.

- Don't smoke.

- Avoid "ums" and don't fidget.

- Be alert to signals to wind it up.

- Remain seated at the end of the interview. Continue to look at interviewer. Don't remove your microphone. The camera may still be on. You'll be told when to move, and your microphone will be removed for you.

PRESS CONFERENCES

Call a press conference when:

- You have news. Hard news.
- When you want to reach all the news media at the same time.
- When you want to give the media the opportunity to ask questions as a group rather than as individuals.
- When you want to be assured of radio and television coverage.

1. The time for press conferences

The best time for a press conference is between 9 a.m. and 1 p.m. The earlier the hour the more likely you will get into the paper and on radio and television that day. Radio, being more immediate, will get the story on faster.

Unexpected disasters will keep the press away.

Bigger stories breaking the same day may keep you from getting the space or air time you'd like.

2. Controlling the press conference

- Make the space comfortable and convenient.
- Start on time.
- Make provisions for time and space following the conference so that key speakers may be interviewed and filmed individually.
- Be sure all your people are well briefed.

- Control the question and answer period (see chapter 10).
- Don't send out negative signals when one of your group is speaking (shaking head, shrugging shoulders).
- Make no character references.
- Don't refer to the sex of members of the press.
- Keep the questions on topic. Be prepared for off-topic questions.
- Summarize at the end of the question period.
- Back up with print support material.

TELEPHONE INTERVIEWS

More and more radio interviews are done by telephone.

- Beware. If you get a phone call from a radio station, determine immediately if you are being taped or are on the air.
- Determine immediately what the purpose of the interview is.
- If you are unprepared, tell them you'll call back in 10 minutes. Prepare yourself and call back.
- Eliminate office noise. Take other phones off the hook. If it is live, turn your own radio off.
- Sit up squarely in your chair. An assertive posture makes for an assertive confident voice.
- Project the voice. Speak clearly and slowly.
- Make answers short and concise.

WHEN IT'S BAD NEWS

When you have good news, you wonder why the media isn't interested. When you have bad news, you wish they weren't. After the crisis occurs is not the time to consider what you should do. Yet, we have been called in after the oil well blows, after the fire, after a three million dollar loss and, unfortunately, after the wrong things have been said or written to the media. The time to deal with a crisis is before it happens. When it does happen, you know the press will cover it. You want to be prepared so that your story is told accurately.

1. What is a crisis?

Crisis can mean different things to different people, different companies. Crisis can be a decisive or crucial time, stage, or event. It can be a time of great danger or trouble with the possibility of bad consequences to follow. Crisis can be external or internal, local or national.

All crisis have things in common.

- They affect large numbers of people.
- They have the possibility of future liability for the organizations concerned.
- They are of ongoing interest to the media.

2. Be prepared

There's no excuse for being caught off guard. Written procedures and plans should be in place detailing what to do and how to do it. Everyone concerned should be familiar with these procedures and plans. The company's representatives may change from crisis to crisis, but the basic plan should remain the same and everyone should know the rules in advance.

3. Project	No matter what business you're in, you can project the kind of crisis that can occur. You can identify hundreds of potential disasters and draw up hundreds of contingency plans. What you must do is determine which crises are most likely to happen. All oil wells have the potential of catching fire, and dead volcanoes come to life.
4. Determining a potential crisis	More subtle signals come from consumers of products, financial analyses, and small brush fires of conflict. Any of these can produce a pattern that forecasts the approach of an explosive crisis.
5. The plan in practice	<ul><li>Anticipate all questions. Prepare answers.</li><li>All top management must be fully aware of the crisis.</li><li>Management must understand the necessity of dealing frankly with the press.</li><li>Assign one person the responsibility for responding to the press. This will assure that the media gets the information they need as quickly and accurately as possible. It also avoids the pitfall of too many voices giving too many versions and making speculations. If the crisis affects several widespread locations you should have a spokesperson at each location. Responses should be carefully coordinated.</li><li>Major crises demand major speakers. If the president isn't heard from, it appears that top management is indifferent and unconcerned. This is particularly true if</li></ul>

there has been loss of life, injuries or threat of greater calamity. Under these conditions a senior spokesperson should be made available.

6. Crisis spokesperson

- Be available to the press.
- Know what you're talking about before the media calls. Be aware of all the facts, all the ramifications, including legal, that affect your company.
- Respond to all media inquiries. Return all phone calls.
- Answer honestly. But don't say more than you have to or want to.
- Don't use company jargon.
- Use simple language. "Vertical integration" and "non-operative" is not simple language.
- During a crisis, journalists other than your usual contacts may be assigned to the story. Provide them with background material on your company. At the same time keep your regular contacts advised on the material you're giving the crisis reporters.
- Provide 24 hour contact service. This will mean giving the press your home phone number. Family members must be prepared to answer the phone in a businesslike manner and keep personal calls short. Install another line if necessary.
- Crises demand keeping cool. No matter what the question or the reporter's attitude, you must remain calm.

- Don't ask for favors. But don't hesitate to let them know promptly if you or anyone in your company has been grossly misquoted or if the reporting has been seriously inaccurate. Confine your comments to the accuracy of the information. Remain positive and cooperative.
- If the crisis involves more than one segment of your company or more than one company set up a "command communication center." This assures that the same information is being given to the media by everyone involved.
- Keep top management informed in writing about which reporters have been talked to and what has been said.
- Employees should be informed about the spokesperson policy. They should be kept up-to-date as much as possible. Rumors and rumblings internally can be detected and exploited by the press.
- Don't lay the blame.
- Don't speak for others, e.g., "I understand the government means to give support . . . ."

14

CONSENSUS COMMUNICATION AND PARLIAMENTARY PROCEDURE

Group discussion and planning depend on interdependence. Interdependence results in a proliferation of meetings. Taking an effective part in group discussion is a specialized and difficult skill. Most of us are more eager to prove ourselves right and someone else wrong than to build a group opinion that would be nearer the truth than the guess of an individual member.

The average person is more interested in carrying through a pet project than in helping formulate a course of action that represents the mature judgment of the group. Even the most intelligent person forms judgments hastily and clings to them tenaciously. Prejudices and pre-formed opinions prevent coming to a consensus.

REACHING A CONSENSUS

1. **Attitude**	Have a clear understanding of the purpose of group discussion. Have a constructive attitude toward the other members of the group. Recognize your own handicaps in discussion proceedings.
2. **Purpose**	The purpose of group discussion is to reach a consensus of opinion or to formulate a plan. It is *not* to win an argument or effect a compromise.
3. **Consensus represents the best**	In order that consensus may represent the best of the total group, each group member should come to a discussion with a tentative opinion. What is

desired is not the acceptance of one person's opinion but the integration of the thought of the whole group. You should be ready to modify your opinion or discard it altogether if it proves inadequate or ill-advised. Too often, persons with predisposed ideas will not change them. Others have no ideas at all, while others speak glibly adding nothing and wasting time.

4. Attitude toward others in the group

You are not an orator. The others are not your audience. Plain but forceful speech is needed, not oratory. Other members should be regarded as co-workers. Try to understand the points of view of the various members. Find some principle by which divergent opinions can be reconciled. The final decision should represent the best thinking of the group.

5. Attitude toward yourself

In discussions, you must be prepared to overcome your own weaknesses and prejudices. (In debate you're concerned with exploiting the opponent's weaknesses. This attitude does not work in discussion.) You must think of what is best for the company or organization rather than what is best for you. Be prepared with adequate research. Recognize that extremes of conservatism, radicalism, optimism, pessimism, idealism, and materialism are personality traits that are difficult to change in yourself and others. (Many of these traits should be recognized before a person is hired or promoted to decision-making positions.)

6. Faulty reasoning

Discipline is necessary to overcome faults in reasoning. Hasty generalization is the result of thoughtlessness, laziness, and the desire to shine in conversation without effort. Define your terms. False analogy is closely connected with hasty generalization. The tendency to reduce individuals to categories is extremely dangerous. It's safer to treat persons, things, and ideas related to others by some principle of fundamental resemblence. Carelessness is the greatest obstacle to good reasoning. For any phenomenon there is usually a chain of causation rather than a simple cause. Poor listening habits also lead to faulty reasoning.

7. Forming a tentative opinion	Make a careful appraisal of what you already know and think about the subject. Distinguish accurately between knowledge and opinion and between reasoned opinion and prejudice.

- Collect material on which to base your judgment.
- Test and weigh this material.
- Give it time to mature and take shape.
- Verify the results of this incubation process.
- Organize the results for effective presentation to the group.
- Revaluate before you meet with the group. Is the material true, pertinent, and important? Is what you have to say free of prejudice?

8. Presenting your tentative opinion	• Go to the meeting determined to present your contribution clearly and effectively so that it will be assured a fair hearing.

- Be ready to recognize the element of truth and logic in the opinions of others and cooperate with them in building a group opinion which will include what is best in the opinions of all.
- Present your material in a style suited to the subject, the occasion, and the listeners.
- Address the chair but speak to the group when presenting material. You'll want to analyze the reactions of the group as you speak.
- Not all reactions will be sympathetic to what you have to say. Ask them to hear you out to the end of what you are saying before expressing opposition.

GROUP DISCUSSION
GOOD CONVERSATION

Group discussion formalizes methods of good conversation. In conversation the primary object is pleasure. In discussion the primary object is crystallization of thought. In good conversation everyone contributes. Good conversationalists have vitality of speech. They're not boring. They don't monopolize conversation. They're good listeners, tactful, insightful, and sympathetic.

1. Group discussion chairperson

The duties of the chairperson are:

- Make a clear statement of the question to be discussed.
- Make certain at the outset that the meaning of the terms used are clearly understood and agreed upon by all the members of the group.
- See that basic facts are stated accurately and fully.

- See that discussions of opinion are prevented whenever facts are available.
- Make sure that each side of the question or each interest, if it is a matter of policy, is fully and fairly stated.
- See that each faction is urged to make a real effort to see the question from the opposite point of view.
- See that issues involved are stated in terms of common sense, practicability, and constructiveness rather than of right and wrong.
- See that discussion is kept as definite and practical as possible with examination of specific examples instead of theorizing and generalization.
- See that a very large issue is broken up into its elements. See that these elements are examined separately. See that the elements are examined in relationship to the whole situation.
- Save time by frequent brief summaries and statements of the exact point reached and the next point to be discussed.
- Don't let discussion reach a premature and unsatisfactory conclusion.
- See that no one dominates the discussion and that everyone gets to speak.
- See that the conclusion that is finally reached is stated clearly.
- If any reasonable number disagree with the conclusion, invite them to draw up a minority report

or give them the opportunity to reopen the discussion at a future time.

2. Controlling discussion

To maintain dignity and courtesy the chairperson may:

- Insist all speakers address the chair.
- Restate tactless remarks.
- Regard the rights of each individual and faction.
- Insist on translation of any emotional language into plain terms.
- Refuse to tolerate emotional outbreaks, frivolous or vulgar language.

RULES TO FOLLOW FOR ALL MEETINGS

- Everyone's time is worth money. Don't call a meeting unless you have a purpose. Know exactly what you expect to accomplish and what you expect the participants to do following the meeting. Every meeting should leave the participants better informed or should initiate action.
- Speeches may be given to large numbers. Presentations can be given to as many as can see the material presented. But you should limit meetings to eight to twelve if you want participation and discussion.
- Choose the participants carefully, considering office politics but also considering what you want to accomplish.

- If you want reports or information, notify the presenters well in advance.

- Circulate an agenda well beforehand. You may wish approval or input before a final agenda is decided upon.

- When starting a meeting, restate the objectives of the meeting or the problem(s) to be discussed.

- The person who called the meeting should act as chair or leader. In that role you must keep to the agenda; keep within the time frame set for the meeting; make sure everyone is heard from and that the purpose of the meeting is fulfilled.

- We re-emphasize that follow-ups are important. You can send out a memo outlining the decisions or conclusions reached, or actions to be taken. This not only informs those who need to be informed but acts as a reminder to those who participated.

USING PARLIAMENTARY PROCEDURE

The fundamentals of parliamentary procedure can help you participate or run meetings in an intelligent, decisive matter.

1. Agenda

(a) Opening exercises:
- Call to order, welcome, roll call, etc., by presiding officer
- Be on time
- Check on the quorum especially if controversial items to consider

(b) Reading of minutes:
- Approved as read, corrected, or written
- Reading of the minutes can be dispensed with by majority vote without debate. This means that they are not read at the regular time. If dispensed with, reading can be ordered any time later during the meeting. They should be read at some time.

(c) Reports of officers:
- Corresponding secretary
- Treasurer's financial report
- Other officers, if they have a report

(d) Reports of standing or special committees:
- Standing committees listed in by-laws are usually called on in the order in which they are listed. A motion arising out of an officer's report or a committee's report is taken up immediately.

(e) Unfinished business:
(or business arising from the minutes)
- A question postponed from the last meeting
- Any other unfinished business (secretary should inform president)

(f) New business:
- Correspondence that needs action
- Bills
- Further new business. Member can introduce new items, or can move to discuss any matter on the table.

(g) Announcements:
- The chair may make. or may call on other members to make any necessary announcements. Members may also obtain the floor for such purpose. The date, time, and place of the next meeting should be announced.

(h) Program:
- The program is usually placed at the end of the order of business, but, by special rule, may be received before the minutes are read, or, by suspending the rules, can be received at any time.

(i) Further business:
- Chair asks if there is further business before adjournment.

(j) Adjournment:
- May be done by general consent or by vote.

2. Putting ideas before the meeting:

(a) Obtaining the floor:
- Address the presiding officer by his or her official title.
- Wait for recognition.
- Once you have the floor you may speak and, without special exceptions, no one may interrupt you.

(b) Making a motion:
- All proposals for action by the group must be presented by a motion.
- Begin by saying: "I move that . . . ."
- Make your motion brief and concise.
- If possible, write the motion out ahead of time; the secretary may request a written copy of any motion.

(c) Seconding a motion:
- Before an idea may be discussed it must be seconded.
- A person need not agree with a motion to second it.
- If the chair overlooks the absence of a second, and debate or voting has begun, the second becomes immaterial. Absence

of a second does not affect the validity of the motion's adoption.

(d) Amending the motion:
   - To add to, substitute, or subtract from a motion that someone else has made, but not change it in principle or intent, submit the idea to the group by amending the motion.
   - Vote on the amendment first, then on the motion as amended.

(e) Amend the amendment:
   - Altering the motion can be carried one step further by an amendment to the amendment.
   - This provides a primary and a secondary amendment to the main motion.
   - There may not be more than two such amendments to any motion.
   - Order of voting would be:
        amendment to the amendment
        amendment as amended
        motion as amended

(f) Point of information:
   - If issues become confusing, a person may ask for clarification by requesting a point of clarification from the chair.

(g) Divide the question:
   - A motion may have two or more parts to be considered separately.
   - You may ask that each part be considered separately. This helps clarify the entire motion and keeps only those parts that most benefit the group.
   - This is usually done by general consent as it requires only a majority.

3. Stick to the facts

(a) Point of order:
   - If you feel a violation of parliamentary

procedure exists, call for a point of order to enforce the rules. The chair rules, but is obliged to recognize you and pass on your inquiry to the group.

(b) Appeal from the decision of the chair:
- If you disagree with the decision of the chair, you can appeal.
- It must be done immediately following the ruling and requires a second.
- The chair then states the question and the entire group votes on whether to overrule or sustain the chair.
- Either a majority vote or a tie will sustain the chair.

(c) Order of the day (request to return to agenda):
- If the meeting goes off on a tangent and does not follow the agenda, or order of business, you may remind the chair by calling for orders of the day.
- This requires a two-thirds vote and is put to vote at the discretion of the chair.

(d) Motion to limit a debate:
- To prevent a discussion from dragging on endlessly you can —
  - (i) move to limit each speaker's time,
  - (ii) move to limit the number of speakers,
  - (iii) move to limit the overall time of debate, or
  - (iv) move to close debate at a set time and hold the vote.
- These questions require a two-thirds vote and safeguards the issue as it requires twice as many votes for an issue as against it.

(e) Motion to refer:
- When it is advisable to give further study to a proposal, move that the matter be referred to a committee.

- Include the kind of committee, size, and power in the motion.

(f) How to end a debate:
- "Put the question" or "call for the previous question" will close debate on a pending question.
- This requires an immediate vote with two-thirds majority to close debate.

4. Postponing consideration

(a) Motion to table:
- A move to table the motion means to temporarily put aside the motion. It is not debatable, and may be removed from the table at the same meeting if other business has intervened. It would then be considered dead and would have to be reintroduced on the order paper.

(b) Postpone to a certain time:
- "I move that action on this matter be postponed until . . ." and state time. If carried, the matter is postponed to the time specified, as unfinished business.

(c) Postponed indefinitely:
- Primarily a strategic motion used to reject the main question without incurring a vote on it.

5. Voting on adjournment

(a) Division of the house — record the vote — recount:
- To get a more accurate count than a voice or hand vote, call for the vote to be recorded. A demand of a single member compels the recording or recount, or division.
- This request must be made when the vote is announced.

- The only motions that can change a vote are to reconsider or rescind.

6. Nice to know

(a) What is the quorum in a committee?
- A majority of its members unless otherwise stated in by-laws.

(b) Does a committee have a secretary?
- The chair may act as a secretary, but, in large committees, it is advisable to have someone else keep records.

(c) Can debate be limited in a committee?
- No.

(d) What rights to ex-official members have?
- All the rights of any other member, but none of the obligations.
- Not counted in a quorum, but must be notified of all meetings.

(e) May a motion be withdrawn?
- Yes. If it has not been restated by the chair, the maker of the motion may withdraw it, and it does not appear in the minutes.
- Once a motion has been stated by the chair, it can be withdrawn only by general consent or a majority vote.

(f) How can action already voted on be reconsidered?
- By a move to reconsider the vote.
- This must be done on the same day the vote was taken, and motion to reconsider may only be made by one who voted on the prevailing side.
- In a standing committee or special committee, a motion to reconsider a vote may be made any time, regardless of the time that has elapsed. It may be made by anyone who voted with the prevailing side or did not vote at all.

(g) Can a motion be rescinded?

- Any member can move to rescind a motion.
- The motion is in order at any time until action has been taken on the matter.
- The motion to rescind requires a majority vote with previous notice, or a two-thirds vote without notice.
- The motion and action to rescind appear in the minutes of the respective meetings where the action was taken.
- The motion to rescind (repeal/annul) reopens the whole question for discussion.

(h) What is a substitute motion?

- A motion of similar, but different, intent than the pending motion.
- If a substitute motion carries by a majority vote, the first motion is discarded, and the second one becomes the pending question.

15

SPEAKING AND THE NEW TECHNOLOGY

SPEAKING ON THE TELEPHONE

In business telephone calls or telephone conferences are a part of everyday routine. Like radio the voice is all important in telephone communication. Your audience cannot see you. You can't make eye contact. They can't see your gestures. Here are some points to consider to make your use of the phone more efficient.

1. Organize

Before you make a phone call, organize as you would a speech or presentation. Why are you making the call? What do you want to accomplish? Do you know the person you're calling? Is there hostility involved?

2. Agenda

- Write down your agenda. You'll be able to tick off your points as you talk and you won't hang up only to realize you forgot to ask or say something.

- Sit up straight when you talk on the phone. Though unseen, good posture keeps you alert and makes your voice alive and interesting.

- Get rid of all distractions. Focus on the purpose of the call.

- Imagine you are speaking to someone directly across from you. "See" the person you're speaking to. This will give your voice animation and the right amount of volume. Don't tuck the phone under your chin.

- Don't drink, eat, smoke or chew gum when telephoning. Extraneous sounds and inarticulate speech are offensive and create a bad image.

- SMILE! If necessary keep a mirror near the phone and check your smiles.

- Identify yourself when you answer the phone. If the call comes directly to you without an operator or secretary identifying the company, give the company's name as well. Immediate identification encourages callers to state their purpose immediately and eliminates the necessity of asking for you.

- If you're calling, always state the purpose of your call in one sentence. Save the anecdotes for non-business calls.

- Use a wind-up sentence that leaves a clear impression about what you want a person to do, or what you feel is expected of you.

- Because you can't see the facial expression of the person on the other end of the phone, ask questions as you go along to make sure you are being understood. You can summarize after each point you've made. Allow the other person to ask questions.

- If you're calling an organization you're not familiar with, locate the individual who can handle the matter before launching into a complete explanation. If you don't, you may find yourself repeating your story over and over. Ask who is in charge of whatever is the main purpose of your call.

- When you reach the person who can help you, get his or her name and use it. The use of names creates attitudes; it transforms anonymous voices into real people. It fixes your listener's attention more closely. Make a note of the name. If you must call again, you have someone specific to contact.

- Be kind to the ear at the other end. Don't bang phones or yell for people to get a call.

- Be conscious of your mood before talking on the phone. The person on the other phone will be quick to detect boredom, exasperation, and every other emotion through your voice.

3. **Para-linguistics**   Listen actively for the unstated messages. These are the verbal equivalent of body language. Listen for the vocal tone and expression. Rather than expressing feelings explicitly through words, the speaker is expressing feelings through vocal tone, vocal expression or lack of expression, vocal energy or lack of energy.

SELLING BY TELEPHONE

The points above should all be followed when selling by telephone. In addition you should consider the following:

- When gathering information, begin with questions that can be answered with "yes" or "no" and follow with the opinion questions.

- Diffuse emotional prospects by allowing them to present their opinion or vent their emotions.

Stop presenting your arguments, no matter how right they may be. If something personal is bothering prospects, don't probe for the problem, just let them express themselves. Then use logic to straighten them out. If you can tell you aren't going to get anywhere today, diplomatically schedule a call for another time.

- Send out verbal messages of encouragement as others are talking. "Is that so." "Great." "Right."
- Concentrate on every word that is being said. Don't plan your responses as the other person is speaking. Your response will be best if you let the other person finish, then proceed.
- Listen with your entire body. Don't fiddle with things on your desk or gaze out the window. You may miss some of the message.
- Don't interrupt.
- Respond to paralinguistic signals by expanding on the thought, restating it in your own words or acknowledging that you understand.
- Never lose your temper. Remain positive.

TELECONFERENCING
More and more businesses and organizations are using video teleconferencing. Video teleconferencing should be used:

- If your target audiences are scattered across the country or abroad.

- If you have a total target audience of 200 or more.

- If your aggregate audience size can be grouped into 25 people or more per location.

- If feedback from your audience is of critical importance to those presenting the information and those listening on the network.

- If the information is technical, detailed or full of facts or figures.

- If you need to illustrate important points through photographs, product demonstration or other visual aids.

- If your speakers need to retain a strong and visible presence among your audience.

- If you want to motivate or train your audience.

- If you wish to meet with your target audience often on a scheduled basis.

- If you can schedule your meeting at least two months in advance.

- If the costs of transportation and accommodation to bring personnel to a central meeting location are far more than the cost of video teleconferencing.

TELEMEETINGS

In telemeetings participants gather in specially equipped, relatively small conference rooms at usually no more than two sites. They talk back and forth via two-way video and two-way audio watching monitors (TV screens). One screen shows the people you're talking to while the other shows the outgoing signal, you and the people in the room with you. The advantages are:

- Verbal interaction with people miles away.
- Time and money saved in transportation and accommodation.
- More efficient than in the flesh meeting. Everyone must be prepared. Meetings must observe a time limit.

1. **Preparation for telemeetings**

- Agendas should be drawn up well in advance and circulated at both ends.
- Go to the telemeeting conference room at least 15 minutes before air time. Familiarize yourself with the setting.
- If you are working in a telemeeting facility where you run the controls, familiarize yourself well in advance. A control panel will allow you to select which camera is to be used. Typically one camera will focus automatically on whoever is speaking; another can be directed at someone standing at the end of the table or showing charts or graphics; still another, in the ceiling, can focus on objects on the conference table.
- With most systems only one person can talk at a time. Being prepared and confident is very important. Hidden agendas, reservations or hesitancy will be very apparent to the viewers of the monitor.
- If you can see yourself on the monitor, don't look. You'll get so caught up in how you look you'll lose the focus of what you want to say.

VIDEOTAPING PRESENTATIONS

When you want to disseminate information to a large number of people but don't want to bring them together for a meeting, you can videotape. Videotaping doesn't allow for immediate feedback or interaction. Use it only when:

- You want a large number of people to receive the same information.
- When the information should be viewed again and again.
- When the strong personal presence of the presenter adds credence and builds confidence in the message.
- When illustration through visual aids is needed to communicate the information.
- When the presenter or speaker has the ability to project an image that will motivate. (Video viewing of motivational messages by chain store staffs has proven to be a strong pre-sale tool if the speaker has good communication skills.)
- When you can schedule simultaneous viewings followed by discussion with the results being forwarded to central locations at a prescheduled time.
- When the cost of video teleconferencing is prohibitive.
- If immediacy is not relevant.

LIGHTS! CAMERA! ACTION!

When you use video teleconferencing or videotaping, you're revealing yourself through the body and the voice. The camera selects what the audience will see. In the chapter on meeting the media, we discuss grooming and dress for television. Here are additional points to consider: .

- Your body and voice should be alert and vital. During videotaping you may find yourself losing vitality. Consciously keep your posture and voice strong. The camera will pick up lethargic body language which translates as bored to viewers. Focus attention on other speakers and appear to be listening attentively.

- When videotaping as a single performer you must communicate with the camera. Do not imagine you're talking to your total audience. Communicate with *one* person. Think of that person as being just inside the lens of the camera. Be conversational but keep the voice alive. Let your communication show in your eyes. Your viewers will be watching your eyes.

- If you're reading your text, follow what we say in chapter 11.

- If you're using a teleprompter, make sure it is very near the camera lens so that your eye contact is camera contact and not off to one side. Rehearse with the teleprompter. Rehearse as often as necessary to make it appear that you're talking not reading. (President Ronald Reagan is the best example of a good teleprompter reader. Prime time news anchors do it well every day.)

- Whether taking part in a teleconference or a videotaping don't let your eyes wander out of the picture over to the supporting technicians.

- Answers given with your head down translate as evasive or sneaky on television. The direct look at the camera or a fellow speaker makes you appear open and honest.

16

THE ART OF LISTENING

The other side of speaking effectively is listening effectively. People often assume in advance that what is said will
be uninteresting. They mentally criticize the delivery
instead of listening to the message.

They pretend to be attentive while actually thinking
about something else. They react with opposition to an
idea instead of listening. They remain silent when the
speaker is unclear. They tune out when the message is
technical. They concentrate on details and miss main ideas.

They try to take notes on everything said. They allow
prejudice against certain words or phrases to block recep-
tivity. They let the mind wander.

LISTENING IN BUSINESS

Depending on your role, you will be listening for different
things.

As a subordinate — you listen for orders and instructions.
You are an information processor. You must get the facts.

- Take concise notes.
- Question for clarification.
- Paraphrase for reinforcement.
- Review instructions immediately.

As a peer — you listen to share information, to reach
mutual decisions, to make cooperative plans, and to problem solve. You must be an evaluative listener, working as a
team member. Listening with an open mind is most important in this role.

As a superior — you are listening to gather feedback. An
authoritative, judgmental attitude discourages feedback.
You must listen with an attitude that will invite honesty.
You don't want subordinates telling you what they *think*

you want to hear. You need honest feedback in order to understand potential problem areas, to evaluate progress, and formulate future plans. Hear the speaker out, ask questions that give you the full picture. Listen critically to what is being said and what is not being said.

As a representative of your company — you must listen sensitively to what you are being told, as well as what you can sense. You are seeking knowledge that others may not want to give you directly. You are listening to discover knowledge of the market, opportunities for you and your company, and public opinion.

1. Message received	Objective listening requires effort. In business communication listening is an important skill. From the message comes the action. If the message has not been clearly understood, the resulting action will not be what the message demanded.
2. Good listening habits	• *Get ready to listen.* Stand or sit where you can hear easily. If necessary, shut doors, take no phone calls. Focus your whole attention on the speaker. Maintain eye contact. Free your mind of bias or prejudice. Resolve to hear what is being said no matter how much you may disagree. Keep cool. Hear the person out.
	• *Begin with the first word and listen continuously.* Because you can think faster than a person can speak, you let your mind consider what is being said, but don't let your attention wander or you may miss an important point.
	• *Listen for the central idea.* You should be able to repeat the central ideas at the end of a listening period. If you listen only for facts or

illustration, you may miss the main points.

- *Relate the subordinate ideas to the central idea.*
  If the speaker has given thought to the presentation, this is relatively easy. If not, you may have to work for it.
- *Be a responsible listener.*
  Keep alert, continue to pay attention, let the speaker have the benefit of your feedback, even if it is not vocalized but is in your face, body, and eyes.
- *Pay more attention to what is being said rather than the way in which it is spoken or how the speaker looks.*
  Facts and ideas are more important than grammar, gestures or garb of the speaker.

3. Critical listening in business

To listen critically is to discriminate rather than to accept gullibly. A critical listener should form the habit of asking:

(a) What is meant by the words used?
(b) What is the motive or purpose?
(c) What has been omitted?
(d) Why should I believe what is being said?
(e) What makes the statements significant?

A GOOD COMMUNICATOR MAKES LISTENING EASIER BY:

- Having enthusiasm for the subject.
- Having vocal variety.

- Presenting a physical presence that demands attention.
- Enunciating clearly.
- Never speaking down to the audience.
- Using language and terminology that the audience understands.
- Being clear and concise. Avoiding jargon and gobbledygook.
- Designing what is said to be of particular interest to the listener or listeners.
- Stating the main points clearly.
- Presenting strong support to the main points.
- Using transitions that move the listener through what is being said.
- Staying on track.
- Summarizing frequently.
- Anticipating what the audience wants to know and answering those questions within the speech, presentation or conversation.
- Reading the reaction of the audience while speaking and responding to it.

All of these points are covered in this book.

APPENDIX 1

REDUNDANCIES IN SPEAKING AND WRITING

The word or words in parenthesis should be deleted.

(a bolt of) lightning
(a distance of) ten yards
(a) myriad (of) sources
(absolute) guarantee
(absolutely) essential
(absolutely) sure
(actual) experience
add (an additional)
(advance) planning
(advance) reservations
(advance) warning
all meet (together)
alongside (of)
(already) existing
aluminum (metal)
(and) moreover
(as) for example
ask (a question)
(as to) whether
(as) yet
(at a) later (date)
(at) (about)
at (the) present (time)
at (12) noon
at (12) midnight
at some time (to come)
(awkward) predicament
(baby) boy was born
bald (-headed)
(basic) fundamentals
blend (together)
bouquet (of flowers)
(brief) moment
burn (down)

burn (up)
(but) (however)
(but) (nevertheless)
came (at a time) when
cancel (out)
(chief) protagonist
climb (up)
(close) proximity
(close) scrutiny
(cold) facts
collaborate (together)
combine (together)
commute (back and forth)
(complete) monopoly
(completely) destroyed
(completely) filled
consensus (of opinion)
continue (on)
(continue to) remain
curiously (enough)
(current) fad
(current) trend
(currently) being
dates (back)
(definite) decision
descend (down)
(different) kinds
(difficult) dilemma
(direct) confrontation
do (over) (again)
drop (down)
during (the course of)
dwindled (down)
each (and every)

earlier (in time)
either (and/or both)
(empty) space
(end) result
enter (in)
equal (to one another)
eradicate (completely)
(established) fact
estimated at (about)
estimated (roughly) at
(every) now and then
(exact) opposites
face (up to)
(false) pretenses
(fellow) classmates
few (in number)
filled (to capacity)
(finally) ended
(first) began
first (of all)
follow (after)
for (a period of) 10 days
(foreign) imports
forever (and ever)
(free) gift
(free) pass
(future) plans
gather (together)
(general) conclusion
(general) custom
(general) public
(glowing) ember
golden (wedding) anniversary
(grand) total
(guest) speaker
had done (previously)
(hard) facts
heat (up)
(hostile) antagonist
(hot) water heater
I (myself personally)
indicted (on a charge)
(integral) part
introduced (a new)
introduced (for the first time)
(invited) guests

(ir)regardless
is (now) pending
join (together)
(just) exactly
(just) recently
kneel (down)
last (of all)
lift (up)
(local) residents
look back (in retrospect)
lose (out)
(major) breakthrough
(mass) media
may (possibly)
mean it (sincerely)
(mental) telepathy
merged (together)
meshed (together)
(midway) between
might (possibly)
mix (together)
(mutual) cooperation
my (personal) opinion
(native) habitat
(natural) instinct
never (at any time)
never (before)
(new) beginning
(new) bride
(new) construction
(new) record
(new) recruit
no trespassing (allowed)
none (at all)
(null and) void
off (of)
(official) business
officiated (at the ceremony)
(old) adage
(old) cliche
(old) pioneer
(old) proverb
(one and the) same
(originally) created
over (and done with)
(over) exaggerate

over (with)
(pair of) twins
(partially) damaged
(partially) destroyed
(passing) fad
(past) experience
(past) history
(past) memories
(past) records
permeate (throughout)
penetrate (into)
(perfect) ideal
period (of time)
(personal) charm
(personal) friendship
(personal) opinion
(pitch) black
pizza (pie)
plan (ahead)
(possibly) might
postponed (until later)
(pre-)plan
(pre-)recorded
(present) incumbent
(private) industry
probed (into)
proceed (ahead)
protest (against)
protrude (out)
(rate of) speed
recur (again)
refer (back)
reflect (back)
repeat (again)
reply (back)
reported (to the effect) that
revert (back)
rose (to his feet)
(rough) rule of thumb

(rustic) (country)
(same) (identical)
(separate) entities
share (together)
since (the time when)
skipped (over)
soaked (to the skin)
(specific) example
spell out (in detail)
stacked (together)
start (out)
started (off) with
(still) persists
(still) remains
strangely (enough)
(suddenly) collapsed
(suddenly) exploded
sufficient (enough)
(sum) (total)
summer (season)
swoop (down)
(sworn) affidavits
talking (out loud)
(temporary) reprieve
(therapeutic) treatment
(thorough) investigation
together (at the same time)
(true) facts
2 a.m. (in the morning)
undergraduate (student)
(underground) subway
(unexpected) surprise
(unintentional) mistake
(usual) custom
(when and) if
whether (or not)
written (down)
(young) foal
(young) lad

APPENDIX 2

CLICHES AND
OVERWORKED PHRASES

A
age before beauty
all that glitters is not gold
almighty dollar
at first blush
at loose ends
at this juncture

B
back to the drawing board
basically
bat out of hell
bee in her bonnet
believe you me
better late than never
between a rock and a
    hard place
between you, me, and the
    lamp post
bird in the hand
bite the bullet
blanket of snow
blood is thicker than water
blow hot and cold
blow your top
blushing bride
bolt from the blue
bone to pick
born with a silver spoon
bottom line
break the ice
break your neck
bright-eyed and bushy-tailed
bring home the bacon
bull by the horns
bundle of nerves
burn the midnight oil

burn your bridges
bury the hatchet
busman's holiday
busy as a bee
by the same token

C
can of worms
can't make head nor tail of
cash on the barrel
cast your pearls before swine
chip off the old block
clean as a whistle
clear as a bell
clear as crystal
clear as mud
clearing the decks
coals to Newcastle
cock-and-bull story
cold as ice
consensus of opinion
    (redundant as well as
    tiresome)
conspicuous by his absence
cool as a cucumber
could care less
credibility gap
cut the mustard

D
dead giveaway
dirty old man
don't put all your eggs in
    one basket
down my alley
draw the line
drink like a fish

drop in the bucket
drown his sorrow
drunk as a skunk
dull as dishwater
dyed in the wool

E
each and every
eager beaver
early on
easier said than done
eh?
eyeball to eyeball
eyes like saucers

F
fair sex
far be it from me
far cry
feather in his cap
feel his oats
few and far between
few well-chosen words
fill the bill
filthy lucre
first and foremost
fish out of water
flat as a pancake
flat on your back
flip your lid
fly-by-night
fly in the ointment
fly off the handle
foregone conclusion
foreseeable future
for the pure and simple
    reason
for all intents and purposes
fresh as a daisy
fresh out of
frozen stiff
frying pan into the fire

G
garden variety
get your dander up
gild the lily

give a piece of your mind
glad rags
gone to seed
good as gold
goose that laid the golden egg
go the whole hog
go to pieces
got up on the wrong side of
    the bed
green as grass
green with envy
grin like a Cheshire cat
gum up the works

H
hair of the dog
hand to mouth
handwriting on the wall
hang in there, baby
happy as a lark
hard as nails
hard row to hoe
has a screw loose
has-been
HAVE A NICE DAY
have another think coming
haven't seen you in a
    coon's age
head over heels
heart of gold
hem and haw
herculean task
high on the hog
hit the nail on the head
hit the sack
hit your head against a
    stone wall
holier than thou
honestly
hook, line, and sinker
hook or crook
horse of a different color
hungry as a bear

I
I can't believe I ate the whole
    thing

I don't know why I have been
    asked . . . I haven't really
    prepared anything
I want to leave you with
this*
if the shoe fits
ignorance is bliss
I'll buy that
in a tight spot
in cahoots with
in full swing
in no uncertain terms
in one ear and out the other
in one fell swoop
in summary*
in this day and age
irons in the fire
it goes without saying
it will all come out in the wash

K
keep body and soul together
kill two birds with one stone

L
last but not least
last straw
leave in the lurch
left-handed compliment
let it all hang out
let's face it
let the cat out of the bag
let your hair down
light as a feather
like a bump on a log
limp as a rag
lips are sealed
lit up like a Christmas tree
live and let live
live high off the hog
live it up
live off the fat of the land

lock, stock, and barrel
long time no see
look a gift horse in the mouth
lose your marbles
lose your shirt
lucky stiff

M
mad as a wet hen
make a clean breast of it
make a long story short/
    longer
make a mountain out of a
    molehill
make ends meet
make hay while the sun
    shines
method in his madness
mind your p's and q's
misery loves company
moot point/question
more easily said than done
more than meets the eye
more than she bargained for
more the merrier
motley crew

N
nagging headache
neck of the woods
needle in a haystack
needless to say
neither fish nor fowl
never a dull moment
never too late
new lease on life
nipped in the bud
no great shakes
no man in his right mind
nose out of joint
nose to the grindstone
no strings attached

*Can be used, but don't overuse.

not a leg to stand on
not by a long shot
not enough sense to come in
    out of the rain
nothing to sneeze at
not worth a Continental
not worth the paper it's
    written on
no way
now (as a transition)

O
okay
old as Methuselah
old stomping/stamping
    ground
on cloud nine
one foot in the grave
on his last legs
on pins and needles
on the spot
on top of the world
other fish to fry
out in left field
out of sight, out of mind
over a barrel

P
pass the buck
pass the time of day
penny for your thoughts
perish the thought
pet peeve
picture of health
pillar of society
play both ends against the
    middle
play it by ear
play your cards right
poor as a church mouse
powers that be
pretty as a picture
pull the wool over his/her
    eyes

pull your own weight
pull yourself together
pure and simple
pure as the driven snow
put a bug in his ear
put on the dog
put on your thinking cap
put your heads together
put that in your pipe and
    smoke it
putting in his/her hands
put your cards on the table
put your foot in your mouth

R
rack your brain
raining cats and dogs
rake over the coals
ran circles around
read the riot act
really and truly
red as a beet
right
ring true
ripe old age
roll out the red carpet
rose-colored glasses
rub the wrong way
run-of-the-mill
run up a red flag

S
sad to say
same wavelength
scenario
see my way clear
sell her a bill of goods
sell like hotcakes
set the world on fire
seventh heaven
shadow of a doubt
shake a leg
shoot the breeze
short and sweet

sight for sore eyes
sincerely
sink or swim
sitting pretty
six of one and half-dozen
  of the other
skin and bones
slowly but surely
small world
snake in the grass
snowed under
sock it to me
soft as snow
so help me Hannah
so on and so forth
speaking off the top of
  my head
spread yourself too thin
square meal
square peg in a round hole
stand on your own two feet
start from scratch
steal your thunder
stick-in-the-mud
stick to the ribs
stick to your guns
stick your neck out
stiff upper lip
straight and narrow
straight from the horse's
  mouth
strange as it seems
strange but true
strike your fancy
strong as an ox
stubborn as a mule
stuffed shirt

T
take it easy
tell tales out of school
thank you (at end of speech)

that type of thing
that's it in a nutshell
thick-skinned
things like that
think tank
through thick and thin
throw in the towel
tidy sum
time hangs heavy
time is of the essence
time was ripe
tit for tat
today I am going to speak
  about
tongue in cheek
too funny for words
too many irons in the fire
took the words right out of
  my mouth
tooth and nail
to recapitulate
to string along
to the bitter end
touch with a ten-foot pole
tough act to follow
tough as nails
true blue
true facts (facts are true)
turn a deaf ear
turn over a new leaf
turn up your nose

U
unaccustomed as I am to
  public speaking
um

W
warm as toast
water over the dam
way out
wear and tear
wee small hours
what a way to go

white as a sheet
whole ball of wax
without further ado
wishy-washy
with bated breath

Y
you know
you'd better believe it
your guess is as good as mine
you're pulling my leg

APPENDIX 3
SAMPLE TELEVISION INTERVIEW

The following is an example of a brief television interview that illustrates how to handle less than friendly questions. The interviewee is a real estate executive. The comments on the left explain what the interviewee did correctly in answering the questions.

	Interviewer:	You people have locked home buyers into high interest rate mortgages. And now people are losing their homes. What are you going to do about it?
Clarifies the question	Interviewee:	By you people, do you mean professional realtors?
	Interviewer:	Why, yes. You sell the houses.
Corrects misinformation	Interviewee:	We do, indeed. But we do not set mortgage interest rates. Banks and trust companies do that. Realtors try to sell real estate at the best price for the seller and the buyer. Financing is arranged by the buyer through the bank or trust company.
	Interviewer:	But you sold houses at high interest rates. Now interest rates have dropped. What are you going to do about those people who bought houses with mortgages of 18%?
Gives background & illustration	Interviewee:	A mortgage is a contract. If you signed a mortgage at 12% for two years and after one year the rate went to 18% you would be very unhappy if your mortgage of 12% went up to 18%. However, most real estate . . . .

	Interviewer:	You're telling me that realtors have no compassion for the individual once they have made a sale. Don't you think . . . .
Handles hostility firmly, but friendly	Interviewee:	On the contrary . . . please allow me to finish. Realtors look upon their clients as lifelong clients and are very concerned. Since the recession which has followed the boom years of high interest mortgages, my company, J.W. Realty, has set up a department within the company to advise our clients who bought during those years. We didn't set the mortgage rates . . . but we don't want to see our clients lose the homes we found for them.
Gets the story across		
Reinforces the point		
	Interviewer:	Can you assure me that they will get a lower interest rate on their mortgage?
Is honest	Interviewee:	No, I cannot. But I can assure you that no reliable realtor wants to sell property at a rate that a client cannot afford. At the same time no one can accurately predict economic booms and busts. What may be a realistic rate based on income today may not be tomorrow. Can you predict the next boom in our economy?
Is concerned for the human factor		
Turns question around		

CANADIAN
ORDER FORM
SELF-COUNSEL SERIES

PROVINCIAL TITLES

Divorce Guide
❑ B.C. 9.95 ❑ Alberta 9.95 ❑ Saskatchewan 12.95
❑ Manitoba 11.95 ❑ Ontario 12.95

Employer/Employee Rights
❑ B.C. 7.95 ❑ Alberta 6.95 ❑ Ontario 6.95

Incorporation Guide
❑ B.C. 14.95 ❑ Alberta 14.95 ❑ Manitoba/Saskatchewan 12.95 ❑ Ontario 14.95

Landlord/Tenant Rights
❑ B.C. 7.95 ❑ Alberta 6.95 ❑ Ontario 7.95

Marriage & Family Law
❑ B.C. 7.95 ❑ Alberta 8.95 ❑ Ontario 7.95

Probate Guide
❑ B.C. 12.95 ❑ Alberta 10.95 ❑ Ontario 11.95

Real Estate Guide
❑ B.C. 8.95 ❑ Alberta 7.95 ❑ Ontario 8.50

Small Claims Court Guide
❑ B.C. 7.95 ❑ Alberta 7.50 ❑ Ontario 7.50

Wills
❑ B.C. 6.50 ❑ Alberta 6.50 ❑ Ontario 5.95
❑ Wills/Probate Procedure for Manitoba/Saskatchewan 5.95

PACKAGED FORMS

Divorce Forms
❑ B.C 11.95 ❑ Alberta 10.95 ❑ Saskatchewan 12.95
❑ Manitoba 10.95 ❑ Ontario 14.95

Incorporation
❑ B.C 14.95 ❑ Alberta 14.95 ❑ Saskatchewan 14.95
❑ Manitoba 14.95 ❑ Ontario 14.95 ❑ Federal 7.95
❑ Minute Books 17.95
❑ Power of Attorney Kit 9.95

Probate
❑ B.C. Administration 14.95 ❑ B.C. Probate 14.95
❑ Alberta 14.95 ❑ Ontario 15.50
❑ Rental Form Kit (B.C., Alberta, Saskatchewan, Ontario) 4.95
❑ Have You Made Your Will? 5.95
❑ If You Love Me Put It In Writing – Contract Kit 14.95
❑ If You Leave Me Put It In Writing – B.C. Separation Agreement Kit 14.95

Interim Agreement
❑ B.C. 2.50 ❑ Alberta 2.50 ❑ Ontario 2.50

Note: All prices subject to change without notice.
Books are available in book and department stores, or use the order form below. Please enclose cheque or money order (plus sales tax where applicable) or give us your MasterCard or Visa number (please include validation and expiry dates).
-✂--

(PLEASE PRINT)
Name _____
Address _____
City _____ Province _____
Postal Code _____
❑ Visa/ ❑ MasterCard Number_____
Validation Date_____ Expiry Date _____
If order is under $20.00, add $1.00 for postage and handling.
Please send orders to:
SELF-COUNSEL PRESS
1481 Charlotte Road
North Vancouver, British Columbia   V7J 1H1

❑ Check here for free catalogue.

SELF-COUNSEL PRESS INC.
ORDER FORM

NATIONAL TITLES   04/89

_____	Aids to Independence	11.95
_____	Arrested! Now What?	7.95
_____	Asking Questions	7.95
_____	Assertiveness for Managers	9.95
_____	Basic Accounting	6.95
_____	Be a Better Manager	8.95
_____	Between the Sexes	8.95
_____	Business Etiquette Today	7.95
_____	Business Guide to Effective Speaking	6.95
_____	Business Guide to Profitable Customer Relations	7.95
_____	Business Writing Workbook	9.95
_____	Buying and Selling a Small Business	7.95
_____	Design Your Own Logo	9.95
_____	Entrepreneur's Self-Assessment Guide	9.95
_____	Every Retailer's Guide to Loss Prevention	15.95
_____	Exporting From the United States	12.95
_____	Family Ties That Bind	7.95
_____	Financial Control for the Small Business	6.95
_____	Financial Freedom on $5 a Day	8.95
_____	Fit After Fifty	8.95
_____	Franchising in the U.S.	6.95
_____	Fundraising for Non-profit Groups	5.50
_____	How You Too Can Make a Million in the Mail Order Business (Washington & Oregon)	9.95
_____	Immigrating to Canada	14.95
_____	Immigrating to the U.S.A.	14.95
_____	Keyboarding for Kids	7.95
_____	Learn to Type Fast	11.50
_____	Managing Stress	7.95
_____	Margo Oliver's Cookbook for Seniors	9.95
_____	Marketing Your Product	12.95
_____	Marketing Your Service	12.95
_____	Mobile Retirement Handbook	9.95
_____	Newcomer's Guide to the U.S.A.	12.95
_____	Parent's Guide to Teenagers and Suicide	8.95
_____	Planning for Financial Independence	11.95
_____	Practical Time Management	6.95
_____	Radio Documentary Handbook	8.95
_____	Ready-to-Use Business Forms	9.95
_____	Small Business Guide to Employee Selection	6.95
_____	Start and Run a Profitable Beauty Salon	14.95
_____	Start and Run a Profitable Consulting Business	12.95
_____	Start and Run a Profitable Craft Business	10.95
_____	Start and Run a Profitable Restaurant	10.95
_____	Start and Run a Profitable Retail Business	12.95
_____	Starting a Successful Business on the West Coast	12.95
_____	Taking Care	7.95
_____	Travelwise	7.95
_____	Upper Left-Hand Corner	10.95
_____	Wise and Healthy Living	9.95
_____	Working Couples	5.50

STATE TITLES — WASHINGTON AND OREGON

(Please indicate which state edition is required)

Divorce Guide
☐ Washington (with forms) 12.95   ☐ Oregon 12.95

Employer/Employee Rights
☐ Washington 5.50

Incorporation and Business Guide
☐ Washington 12.95   ☐ Oregon 11.95

Landlord/Tenant Rights
☐ Washington 6.95   ☐ Oregon 6.95

Marriage & Family Law
☐ Washington 7.95   ☐ Oregon 4.95

Probate Guide
☐ Washington 9.95

Real Estate Buying/Selling Guide
☐ Washington 6.95   ☐ Oregon 3.95

Small Claims Court Guide
☐ Washington 4.50

Wills
☐ Washington 6.95   ☐ Oregon 6.95

PACKAGED FORMS

Divorce
☐ Oregon Set A (Petitioner) 14.95
☐ Oregon Set B (Co-petitioners) 12.95

☐ If You Love Me — Put It In Writing 7.95

Incorporation
☐ Washington 12.95   ☐ Oregon 12.95

Probate
☐ Washington 9.95

☐ Rental Form Kit 3.95

☐ Will and Estate Planning Kit 4.95

All prices subject to change without notice.

✂ —

(PLEASE PRINT)

NAME _____

ADDRESS _____

CITY _____

STATE _____

ZIP CODE _____

Check or money order enclosed

If order is under $20, add $2.50 for postage and handling. Allow six weeks for delivery.

Washington residents add 8.1% sales tax.

Please send orders to:

SELF-COUNSEL PRESS INC.
1704 N. State St.
Bellingham, Washington 98225
☐ Check here for free catalog